Ethics
and Real Estate

DORIS BARRELL,
CRB, CRS, GRI

Dearborn
Real Estate Education

While a great deal of care has been taken to provide accurate and current information, the ideas, suggestions, general principles and conclusions in this text are subject to local, state and federal law and regulations, court cases and any revisions of same. The reader is thus urged to consult legal counsel regarding any points of law—this publication should not be used as a substitute for competent legal advice.

Publisher: Diana Faulhaber
Development Editor: Kristen Short
Managing Editor: Ronald J. Liszkowski
Art Manager: Lucy Jenkins

© 2000 by Dearborn Financial Publishing, Inc.®

Published by Real Estate Education Company®,
a division of Dearborn Financial Publishing, Inc.®
155 North Wacker Drive
Chicago, IL 60606-1719
(312) 836-4400
http://www.dearborn.com

All rights reserved. The text of this publication, or any part thereof, may not be reproduced in any manner whatsoever without written permission from the publisher.

10   9   8

Library of Congress Cataloging-in-Publication Data

Barrell, Doris.
    Ethics and real estate / Doris Barrell.
        p. cm.
    ISBN 0-7931-3847-7
    1. Real estate agents—Professional ethics. 2. Real estate business—Moral and ethical aspects. 3. Business ethics. I. Title.
    HD1382.B372000
    174'.933—dc21
                                                                        00-032330

Table of Contents

Preface		iv
Chapter 1	An Introduction to Ethics	1
Chapter 2	National Association of REALTORS® Code of Ethics	11
Chapter 3	A Blueprint for Decision Making	23
Chapter 4	Ethics and the Real Estate Business	35
Chapter 5	Ethical Dilemmas in Real Estate	47
Glossary		61
Answer Key		66

Preface

The challenge of writing a book on ethics is that there are so many questions and very few answers. When the book is to be used as course material for continuing education classes, the problem is even greater. Students and teachers are looking for answers to the situations presented for case studies. Quizzes require a selection of the "right" answer. Examinations are based on the number of questions answered correctly.

As will be pointed out in the text, ethical dilemmas are often a question of one right versus another right. Who is to say which is the greater right? Every situation requiring an ethical decision will have different circumstances. Clearly defined, objective answers are few and far between. Each case lends itself to a subjective study of all the circumstances involved, the personal involvement of all parties and the impact that today's decision may have on similar situations in the future.

In each chapter of the book, there are questions raised for which the author has given no answers. Hopefully, these questions will provide a basis for serious thought by the person independently studying the text. The questions should provide a basis for active discussion if they are being used in the classroom.

In the quizzes themselves, the author has provided what was in her judgment the right answer. You may agree or disagree with her, but the important thing is that you give serious thought to the question and determine what in your opinion is the most right answer.

ACKNOWLEDGMENTS

Ethics and Real Estate would not have been possible without the thoughtful feedback of real estate instructors. The author wishes to thank the following reviewers for their comments, suggestions and contributions:

- Marie Callas, Iowa Association of REALTORS®, Clive, Iowa
- Susan Davis, America's Best On-Line Real Estate Education, Sequim, Washington
- Judy Wolk, Charleston Trident Association of REALTORS®, Charleston, South Carolina

An Introduction to Ethics

LEARNING OBJECTIVES
After completing this chapter, you will be able to:

✓ Provide a definition of ethics.

✓ Explain traditional sources for motivating ethical behavior.

✓ List sources available for help in making ethical decisions.

KEY TERMS

code of ethics
ethics
Fair Housing Act
morals
multiple listing service (MLS)
Real Estate Settlement Procedures Act (RESPA)
Sherman Antitrust Act
standards of conduct

WHAT ARE ETHICS?

The difficulty with trying to define "ethics" is that it is a bit like trying to lasso a cloud. You can see it, you can almost touch it, but when you try to rope it in, it just slips away.

In the simplest of terms, **ethics** can be defined as dealing with what is fair and right. However, definitions of ethics, ethical behavior, or ethical standards are bound to be subjective. Ethical decisions are often based on present circumstances. Faced with an almost identical situation on a different day, a totally different decision might be reached.

Ethics and Morals

"I know only that what is moral is what you feel good after and what is immoral is what you feel bad after."

—Ernest Hemingway, *Death in the Afternoon*

Although moral and ethical are generally considered to be synonymous, there is a slight difference in meaning. **Moral** tends to be more concerned with the accepted codes for good behavior or sanctions of a community, while ethical implies a higher standard of concern for what is right or fair for all parties involved. A moral decision is more related to feelings; an ethical decision is more related to thinking.

Are Ethical and Legal the Same?

Anyone who has been in the real estate business for a number of years has inevitably faced a dilemma where the legal position is clear-cut, but the ethical one is not. What is right according to the law and what constitutes ethical behavior are not necessarily always the same. The entire concept of a **code of ethics**—a set of principles of conduct—is to achieve a *higher* standard of conduct than that required by law.

Consider the following situation:

Mark J. has a listing on a five-story office building located in a transition area of town. There has been little interest shown in the property, but yesterday Mark received a call from a prospective buyer from out-of-town. Mr. J. Hughes will be coming to see the property tomorrow. He was especially interested after learning that the building is currently fully leased. Mr. Hughes has calculated that by making a down payment of 30 percent, he will be able to cover his debt service plus expenses with a small margin of net profit. By successfully carrying the property for about five years, he will be in a position to completely renovate and sell it for a handsome profit. Mr. Hughes understands that Mark represents the seller, but he considers himself to be an experienced investor and does not feel it is necessary to contract with a buyer agent to represent him.

When Hughes explains his long-range plan, Mark is faced with a dilemma. Hughes's plan relies on the building staying occupied for at least five years. Although the building is fully leased today, Mark is well aware that two tenants occupying two full floors plus half of the ground floor street frontage are planning to move out in about 18 months. As it happens, Mark is representing the two tenants in the leasing negotiations for a new building presently awaiting approval from the city planning commission. Because of the location and present physical condition of the building, it may be very difficult to find new tenants, and there is a strong likelihood that Mr. Hughes would be faced with a significant cash-flow deficiency for some period of time.

When Mark meets with Mr. Hughes tomorrow, he will have a number of choices:

1. Stick with the true fact that the building is fully leased and make no comment about any future plans. After all, nothing has been done in writing and plans could fall through. Besides, Mark is only representing the seller's best interests.

2. Explain to Hughes that there could be a possibility of tenants leaving in 18 months but offer to act as his listing agent for a reduced fee if that should happen.

3. Stress the fact that Mark only represents the seller and strongly advise Hughes to obtain the services of a buyer agent who will hopefully ask the right questions.

4. Justify to himself that he is acting in the best interest of the community to let Hughes proceed with the purchase since he will eventually make an improvement to the property.

Mark has no legal responsibility to inform Mr. Hughes about the present tenant's future plans. Mark is pledged to protect the best interests of his seller client and must make every effort to fulfill his duty to provide the seller with a ready, willing and able buyer.

But Mark is also aware that if the two tenants do move out in 18 months, it will be very difficult to replace them. Mr. Hughes would be faced with a significant cash-flow problem and could end up with the property in foreclosure.

Mark's legal position is crystal clear. His ethical responsibility to his client, to the customer, to the remaining tenants and even to the community as a whole is many shades of gray.

WHAT MOTIVATES ETHICAL BEHAVIOR?

The Family

The first social organization we all belong to is the family. In today's world of extended families, one-parent households, "yours, mine and ours," the traditional mom, dad, three kids and a dog may no longer be the norm. Whatever the makeup, the family—the setting in which we are born and initially raised—sets the pattern for our first sense of what's right and wrong. For example:

> Mom says *"Don't squeeze the cat around the neck! That hurts her and we must always take care of those who depend on us and try not to hurt them."*

> Dad says *"Do not take the fire engine away from your little brother. I know Santa brought it to you, but we must learn to share."*

Family-oriented behavior in the real estate world is most evident in the individual real estate offices. Agents in the same company, even though they are direct competitors, often have a real sense of family and will work together as a team and on many occasions will assist a fellow agent in carrying out a transaction. For example, George, Margaret, Tom and Sally all have listings in Happy Acres subdivision. Although they are each interested in becoming "the" agent for that subdivision, they decide to cooperate in a special "Spring Is Here" open house special. They will split the cost of a large newspaper advertisement directing visitors to all four open houses, yellow and green balloons to decorate each house and fresh daffodils to give away to all the guests.

Margaret is expecting her first child any day now and is finding it difficult to get in and out of her car and to navigate stairs. Sally offers to meet Margaret's clients and the home inspector at the house they have just put under contract and stay there with them until the inspection is completed.

Unfortunately, some agents will carry over bad family-oriented behavior such as selfishly trying to take away a prospective client from another agent, or using a good deed, such as Sally's in the above example, as an excuse to establish a contact with another agent's clients!

The School

The next social organization to contribute to the child's growing sense of ethical behavior and values comes from the day-care center or kindergarten, continuing to first grade on through graduation from high school, and for many young people, advanced education in colleges and universities. Hopefully, the school is teaching ethical behavior such as integrity and honesty. School also provides the opportunity to teach the values of sharing and team work. For example:

Teacher says *"Jack, you must learn to answer the questions on the quiz all on your own. Looking at Susie's paper to get the answers is called cheating and is wrong."*

Coach says *"Every single one of you is an important member of this team. The only way we win is when everyone works together to give their best."*

Negative schoolroom or playground behavior is easily translated into real estate examples:

Sam has completed the principles and practices of real estate course required in his state to obtain a real estate license and is now ready to take the state exam. Sam has never been a good "test taker," however, and plans to send in his brother who has been licensed for five years to take the exam in his place.

In many states, the licensing authorities are now requiring a fingerprint in addition to photo ID for all persons taking the state real estate exam. This came as a result of people like Sam having someone take the exam for them.

Sue has just obtained her real estate license. She is dismayed at the costs involved in getting started and asks her friend Mary if she could use Mary's lockbox key for a while until she starts making money.

Access to properties for sale is usually obtained through use of a lockbox. Each agent is responsible to their company, their local REALTOR® association, and to the clients to maintain exclusive use of their lockbox key. Loaning or sharing a lockbox key is unethical behavior and may result in a fine or revocation of the right to use. Loaning your lockbox key is like loaning someone your homework. The agent is not learning to accept responsibility.

A more positive lesson learned in school is teamwork. Real estate teamwork may be seen in an office when two groups are involved in a listing contest. All the members of each team meet together to send out a mailing or come to the office three evenings a week for cold-calling sessions into neighborhoods where they would like to obtain listings. The team spirit will promote activities that the individuals would probably never do on their own.

Religion

Throughout the centuries religion has played a strong role in defining social behavior within communities. Religions set acceptable standards of moral behavior such as the Ten Commandments, the Golden Rule and principles presented in the Koran. Religions may encourage protection of the poor, the sick, the elderly, the young; they may encourage love and compassion for all. Religions may also teach their followers to put the needs of others ahead of their own.

Ethical standards for behavior based on religion may be found in the following:

The Ten Commandments—the "thou shalls" and "thou shall nots"

The Golden Rule—"Do unto others as you would have them do unto you."

The Koran—strive for the benefit of humanity, not self.

Protecting and promoting the best interests of the client is the hallmark of ethical real estate behavior. Putting the wants and needs of the client ahead of those of the agent is not always as easy as it may sound, however. For example:

Mark's listing at 1423 Hickory Lane has finally sold after nine months of a long and difficult marketing effort. The offer was considerably lower than the asking price but was finally accepted two days ago with terms acceptable to both buyer and seller.

This morning Mark received a call from Jack who told him that he has another offer to present on that property that actually exceeds the original asking price. Mark does not really want to deal with this new offer and is tempted to tell Jack to forget it, that the deal is done, no backups to be considered, and so on, but would that be in the best interest of the client?

Margaret has just listed the home of her best friend Susan. Susan tells her that she really would like Margaret to be the one to sell the house and would be happy to give her an exclusive listing that would not be entered into the **multiple listing service (MLS)**. Margaret is tempted by the prospect of earning both sides of the transaction but realizes that it is much more in Susan's best interest to have the property presented to the larger market available through use of the MLS.

The Law

In a perfect world where everyone grew up in a family where all the highest ideals of honesty and loving care were taught, where children extended that early training in doing the right thing through the educational years and reached adulthood with ethical values firmly instilled, there would be no need for governments and other institutions to step in with laws, rules and regulations, and formalized codes of ethics. Unfortunately, there is no perfect world, and it has been necessary for entities outside the individual to formulate specific guidelines for behavior that must be obeyed or the person violating them will be punished.

The real estate industry is no exception. Consider any of the following congressional acts that establish clear guidelines for the purchase, sale or lease of real estate:

- **Sherman Antitrust Act**—fairness in the marketplace

  A group of real estate brokers met for lunch one day at a local country club. They were overheard discussing the fact that times were difficult and that maybe they should increase the rate of commission that they charged for marketing properties. Just an informal lunch, but with drastic consequences! Discussion of commission rates is price-fixing, which is absolutely forbidden under the Sherman Antitrust Act.

- **Real Estate Settlement Procedures Act (RESPA)**—full disclosure of all costs involved in obtaining financing and closing on a property

  EZMoney Mortgage offered the best deal in town – no money down and a 7 percent interest rate for 30 years!

Unfortunately, the loan officer did "forget" to tell the borrower about the six points to be charged at settlement plus an annual fee of 2 percent of the selling price for private mortgage insurance; plus of course the "normal" lender fees of $1,500 to be paid at closing. EZMoney may soon be out of business for failing to provide the purchaser with a good-faith estimate of all costs in the transaction.

- **Fair Housing Act**—equal treatment for all people

In the 1950s and early 1960s, a few unscrupulous real estate agents would go into a neighborhood telling the present home owners that a member of another race would soon be moving in and they had better sell their homes quickly before the values dropped. This ugly practice, called "blockbusting," was outlawed by civil rights actions in the '60s which also guaranteed the right to purchase anywhere a prospective buyer could afford regardless of race, color, religion, or national origin. Later legislation added the categories of sex, familial status and mental or physical handicap.

WHERE TO FIND HELP IN MAKING ETHICAL DECISIONS

Personal Resources

Real estate agents faced with an ethical dilemma can often draw on their own resources based on their sense of values or moral conduct learned through their own upbringing or education. Discussing the problem with a member of the family, a former teacher or a religious advisor can often help. Sometimes, just talking out the problem with an objective, unbiased listener will lead the way to making an ethical decision.

State Licensing Rules and Regulations

A section on **standards of conduct** is often included in the rules and regulations that are a part of the licensing law in every state. The standards of conduct are similar to a code of ethics but specify behavior that may actually violate license laws. Although ethical decisions are often made that exceed the limitations of state license law, the license law or standards of conduct may provide a good starting place from which to begin the thought process for making the decision.

REALTOR® Code of Ethics

Members of the National Association of REALTORS® are pledged to follow the REALTOR® Code of Ethics. The 17 articles and numerous standards of practice relating to the various articles provide very definitive answers for many ethical questions that may arise between an agent and his or her clients or between two agents. Case interpretations relating to different articles provide real-life examples of actual cases with the corresponding action taken by a hearing panel. Finding a case similar to the problem at hand may assist an agent in making a decision that would ensure that the agent was not in violation of the Code.

Peers or Colleagues

"Been there, done that" has certainly become an overused phrase, but there is still a great deal to be said for experience. A managing broker has probably been involved in, or at least knows of, many of the same problems that face an agent today. Whether an agent is relatively new, or has many years of experience, he or she can still benefit from discussing a problem with someone that has had a similar experience.

Printed Material

Local, state and national REALTOR® associations regularly publish newsletters or magazines containing hypothetical cases and suggested resolutions on ethical matters. Public libraries have indexed references for ethics in both magazine and book form. A quick glance at the headlines of any major newspaper today will provide many examples of ethical dilemmas—but few answers. Specific books on real estate ethics include:

> William H. Pivar and Donald L. Harlan, *Real Estate Ethics: Good Ethics = Good Business,* 3rd ed. (Chicago: Dearborn Financial Publishing, Inc., 1995)

> Deborah H. Long, *Doing the Right Thing: A Real Estate Practitioner's Guide to Ethical Decision Making,* 2nd ed. (Upper Saddle River, New Jersey: Prentice-Hall, Inc., 1998)

Internet

The latest resource for information on ethics and making ethical decisions may be found on the computer through the electronic network of the Internet. Amazon.com and Barnes and Noble both have excellent web sites where entering the subject "ethics" will suggest books on the subject.

Entering "ethics" under "search" in any of the various search engines will provide a great number of suggested books and articles. A few of particular interest are:

> Carter McNamara, "A Complete Guide to Ethics Management: An Ethics Toolkit for Managers" found at www.mapnp.org

> "A Framework for Ethical Decisions" at www.ethics.ubc.ca

> "Institute of Global Ethics" at www.globalethics.org

SUMMARY

Defining ethics is a difficult task but it is generally accepted that ethics are primarily focused on what is right and fair. A code of ethics is described as a formal set of principles of conduct that may actually surpass any legal obligation.

A sense of what is right and wrong is first developed in the home and family environment. Hopefully, a child will continue to develop a sense of proper ethical behavior through experiences in the school environment and through religious beliefs.

Ultimately, the law itself will demand certain aspects of ethical behavior through state regulatory body rules and regulations and federal legislative acts.

There are various resources available to a real estate licensee looking for help in making an ethical decision. Discussion with a trusted colleague may be beneficial. A review of state regulations for standards of conduct or the REALTOR® Code of Ethics can provide specific examples of ethical standards of practice. Printed material provides background material and the Internet makes it possible to research the latest issues and guidelines.

Chapter 1 / An Introduction to Ethics

Quiz

1. An ethical decision is most concerned with

    a. moral behavior standards.
    b. what is right and fair for all parties.
    c. community sanctions.
    d. legal issues.

2. Morals tend to be more concerned with

    a. what is right and fair for all parties.
    b. a specific code of conduct.
    c. accepted codes and sanctions of a community.
    d. the worth of the subject.

3. Even though the law may be very clear, an agent is often faced with making an ethical decision over the disclosure of

    a. property rights.
    b. buyer agency agreements.
    c. listing agreements.
    d. nonmaterial facts relative to the transaction.

4. In the example on page 2, Mark has the greatest legal responsibility to

    a. his seller client.
    b. the customer Hughes.
    c. the present tenants.
    d. the community.

5. The concept of sharing as part of ethical behavior is best learned

    a. at home or school in early childhood.
    b. during high school or college.
    c. by attending church weekly.
    d. through study of real estate law.

6. Robert, who recently immigrated to the U.S., is preparing to take his real estate licensing exam. He knows the material very well, but it takes him much longer to answer questions because English is his second language. His best choice would be to

   a. have a friend take the exam for him.
   b. request an extension of time from the state licensing authority.
   c. take the exam and hope for the best.
   d. retake the principles class and hope to improve his language skills.

7. When an agent attempts to make an ethical decision based on how he or she would want to be treated in the same situation, the agent is most likely relying on

   a. license law rules and regulations.
   b. state agency law.
   c. the Golden Rule.
   d. the Koran.

8. Ethical behavior is often imposed on real estate agents through the law. For example, open and fair trade in the marketplace is regulated by the

   a. Sherman Antitrust Act.
   b. Real Estate Settlement Procedures Act.
   c. Fair Housing Act.
   d. REALTOR® Code of Ethics.

9. Case studies based on actual professional standards hearings that include the findings of a hearing panel are provided to local and state associations by the

   a. state regulatory agency.
   b. state legislative body.
   c. National Association of REALTORS®.
   d. local newspaper archives.

10. Which of the following is NOT a good source of guidance for making an ethical decision?

    a. Advice from a knowledgeable and trusted colleague
    b. REALTOR® Code of Ethics
    c. Internet
    d. General office opinion

National Association of REALTORS® Code of Ethics

2

LEARNING OBJECTIVES
After completing this chapter, you will be able to:

✓ Discuss the factors contributing to the public's negative image of real estate agents.

✓ Describe the original purpose and organization of the National Association of REALTORS®.

✓ Identify the three sections of the REALTOR® Code of Ethics and explain the relationship of the Articles and the Standards of Practice.

✓ Explain how the REALTOR® Code of Ethics is enforced.

KEY TERMS

adverse material defects
arbitration hearing
client
customer
due process
Eastern European Real
    Property Foundation (ERPF)

fiduciary responsibility
Grievance Committee
land agents
mediation
National Association of
    REALTORS® (NAR)
Professional Standards Hearing

REALTOR®
sanctions
Standard of Practice
stigmatized property

PUBLIC PERCEPTION OF REAL ESTATE AGENTS

In the Early Days

"Such a deal I have for you!" Readers of history novels are very familiar with the notorious scams promoted by unscrupulous **land agents** in the 19th century and first part of the 20th. People were lured to California with promises of sunshine, cheap land for sale and beautiful orange groves as far as the eye could see. Unfortunately, the land agent—the person selling the property—left out the part about needing water for those orange groves!

Water was also a problem for land sales on the East Coast; not a lack of water, but too much. That "super deal" on property in Florida sounded perfect—until the new owners arrived to find that their land was under two feet of alligator-infested swamp!

For at least 150 years, the sale of property often involved get-rich-quick schemes, rampant exploitation and total lack of trust by all parties. The only certification to sell real estate in those years might have been a peddler's license, and even that was not required in most states.

State licensing. The actions of unscrupulous land agents led, in part, to a national movement toward mandatory licensing of real estate agents. Each state now has a regulatory body that sets the requirements for licensure within that state. A specific number of hours of classroom study plus passing a written exam is required in addition to passing the official state exam before a license is issued.

Each state also prepares its own set of rules and regulations that generally includes a section on standards of conduct. All licensees within that state must follow these rules and regulations or be subject to reprimand, fine, or loss of license.

Today's View of Real Estate Practitioners

Despite the strict requirements for real estate licenses, there has been a long-standing joke about the low opinion the public has of those who sell real estate. The Gallup Poll has consistently ranked real estate agents around 36th or 37th out of 45 professions or occupations in their annual Honesty and Ethics Poll.

Unfortunately, most contemporary movies have only added to this poor image of real estate agents, who are usually depicted as either money-grubbing cheats or insipid airheads! TV shows and best-seller novels do not do any better than the movies in their portrayal of those who sell real estate.

Working for a sharper image. Following the success of a public awareness campaign originated in California, the National Association of REALTORS® began a similar three-year campaign in 1998. The purpose of this public awareness campaign is to show the public just what real estate agents actually do! Earlier surveys had shown that most people thought their agent merely stuck a sign in the ground, entered some information in some kind of multiple listing system and then sat back and waited for the commission to roll in.

One of the most visible parts of the REALTOR® campaign is the series of dramatized TV ads centered on the theme "You've got a life—we let you live it! We're REALTORS®. Real estate is our life." After one full year of the campaign with the ads appearing on network and cable TV, surveys showed that the public actually had become more aware of the types of services and activities that an agent handles on behalf of their clients in every real estate transaction.

THE NATIONAL ASSOCIATION OF REALTORS®

Getting Started

In 1908 a group of 120 real estate practitioners dedicated to seeing the business of selling real estate become a respected profession founded the National Association of Real Estate Boards, later to become the **National Association of REALTORS® (NAR)** with over 730,000 members today.

The primary purpose of the association was to establish high standards of business practice and professional conduct for real estate practitioners. These early visionaries set goals of honest and competent service to clients and the public in general.

Membership in the association is three-tiered, with each member maintaining membership in local, state and national associations. For many years the local level association was referred to as the "local board" of REALTORS®. In most cases, the local board has now been renamed the "association."

NAR Today

The more than 730,000 members of NAR come from all areas of the real estate industry. The membership is made up of residential and commercial brokers, salespersons, property managers, appraisers, counselors and some other affiliates.

One of the largest growing divisions of NAR is the international division. Each year more and more representatives from other countries attend the NAR annual convention.

Beyond our shores. One of the most interesting results of the dissolution of the former Soviet Union in 1989 was the ability of people to regain private ownership of property. The ability to have an open real estate market where people can buy and sell property has resulted in an emerging real estate industry in many countries.

The **Eastern European Real Property Foundation (EERPF),** started by the National Association of REALTORS® in conjunction with the U.S. Agency for International Development (USAID) in 1995, sends association executives, brokers, and other industry leaders to the countries of Eastern and Central Europe to help them develop a real estate industry with high standards of professional conduct and ethical business practices. One of the first steps taken in each country is to assist the local leaders to develop a code of ethics to be followed by all members of the new organization.

NAR Develops a Code of Ethics

Origin and purpose. The REALTORS® were the first business group outside the professions of law, medicine and engineering to develop a code of ethics. The REALTOR® Code of Ethics was written in 1913 and was first presented as "Rules of Conduct" to be voluntarily adopted by local boards. Compliance with the Code became a mandatory condition of membership in the association in 1924. The Code of Ethics is enforced at the local or state level with guidance on policies and procedures from the national organization.

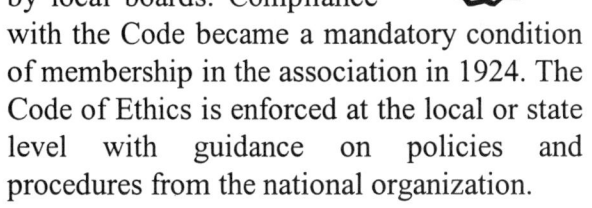

The pledge of REALTORS®. What distinguishes a **REALTOR®** (member of the National Association of REALTORS®) from a real estate licensee is that a REALTOR® is pledged to follow the very strict Code of Ethics and Standards of Practice subscribed to by all members of the association.

Peer process vs. court process. The ultimate goal of the Code of Ethics is to protect the public through the use of an informed peer process as opposed to court litigation. Although occasionally a member of the public argues that peers may not be objective, the process has proved to be a valid one that has saved REALTORS® and members of the public time, money and reputation.

Organization of the Code

The Preamble. The powerful opening paragraphs of the Preamble to the Code of Ethics were written in 1913 and still provide a source of inspiration and pride to thousands of new members. The principles contained in the Preamble are considered to be aspirational only and are not subject to enforcement. They do, however represent the highest ideals and ethical standards of practice that a real estate professional today strives to make a part of his or her daily practice.

The Articles. There were originally 23 separate Articles in the Code of Ethics. In 1995 6 were eliminated and their principles added to other articles or included in the preamble. There are now 17 Articles, divided into three sections, each covering one particular aspect of ethical business practice. Articles 1 through 9 are Duties to Clients and Customers, Articles 10 through 14 are Duties to the Public, and Articles 15 through 17 are Duties to Fellow REALTORS®.

The Articles themselves are amended from time to time to conform with changing business practices; for example, the advent of buyer agency in the mid-90s and, more recently, technological changes like the Internet.

Standards of Practice. After studying cases presented for **Professional Standards Hearings** or observing changing business practices within the industry, it is occasionally necessary to provide additional guidance in the interpretation of an Article through a **Standard of Practice.** A Standard of Practice is created to clarify the intent of an Article. Specific examples may be given in the Standard of Practice to illustrate how the Article is to be interpreted. Although a few Articles have never seemed to need clarification or amplification (for example: Article 13 that says REALTORS® shall not practice law), others have required more specific examples of the intent of the Article. Article 16, which deals with the respect for the agency position of another REALTOR®, currently has 20 different Standards of Practice.

The living document. The Code remains a living document. The Professional Standards Committee of NAR reviews it thoroughly every year. Changes are made when necessary—sometimes through an amendment or addendum, sometimes with an entirely new Standard of Practice.

Enforcement of the Code

Local and state associations are responsible for enforcing the Code of Ethics. NAR provides suggested policies and procedures to be followed to ensure that correct **due process** is followed. Due process establishes set procedures to be followed in all cases to ensure fair treatment for everyone.

Actual case studies of alleged unethical conduct are made available for hearing panels to use as guidelines in cases of a similar nature. No specific sanctions for violations are given since every case would potentially be different, but NAR does provide suggested sanctioning guidelines.

Sanctions range from letters of reprimand or warning, required attendance at an ethics class, fines, probation, suspension, to the ultimate of expulsion from the association.

The Process

Filing the complaint. A member of the general public or a REALTOR® may file a complaint alleging that a REALTOR® has violated one of more of the Articles of the Code of Ethics. A complaint must be registered alleging a violation of one of the 17 Articles themselves, but specific Standards of Practice may be also be cited as further evidence. The complaint is then reviewed by the Grievance Committee.

Grievance Committee. The **Grievance Committee** is made up of REALTOR® members who act in a similar way to a grand jury in the court system. The Grievance Committee reviews a complaint and determines only "if the facts as presented are true, would there be a legitimate complaint." If so, the complaint is then sent forward to a Professional Standards Hearing Panel in the case of an ethics complaint, or to an Arbitration Hearing Panel in the case of an arbitration complaint.

Professional Standards hearing. After a complaint is forwarded to Professional Standards from Grievance, a panel is selected to hear the complaint. Great care is taken to ensure that the panel is not biased toward either complainant or defendant. Both parties are given an opportunity to present their cases along with legal counsel if they so choose. The parties are then dismissed and the panel convenes to determine whether a specific Article has been violated. If it is determined that there has been a violation, an appropriate sanction will be made. The decision may be appealed to the local board of directors.

Due process. NAR provides printed forms and procedural guidelines to ensure that all complainants are handled according to due process. Professional Standards training is also required of all staff and members who are to participate in hearing panels.

Arbitration. Article 17 of the Code requires REALTORS® to arbitrate rather than litigate. Arbitration hearings generally concern commission disputes between brokers. The **Arbitration Hearing Panel** must determine who was the procuring cause of the transaction and reward the amount in dispute accordingly. The decision is not subject to appeal.

Mediation. Just as there is an increasing interest in the use of mediation in the civil courts, **mediation** is also being recommended in real estate arbitration cases. In these cases, a professional mediator assists the parties involved in making their own resolution of the problem but does not make any decision. If mediation fails, the parties may still resort to arbitration.

THE REALTOR® CODE OF ETHICS

The Most Cited Articles

Article 1. Throughout the country, Article 1 is the one most often cited when a complaint is brought against a REALTOR®. Almost two-thirds of all complaints filed cite Article 1 as at least one part of the complaint. Article 1 states that a REALTOR® pledges to maintain an absolute obligation to protect and promote the interests of his or her client. The REALTOR® further pledges to treat all parties to a transaction honestly, whether they are a **client** (the party with whom the agent has a brokerage relationship) or a **customer** (the party to the transaction with whom the REALTOR® has no brokerage agreement).

Any of the 13 Standards of Practice attached to Article 1 may also be cited. Ten of the 13 have been adopted or amended since 1993 when the brokerage relationship of buyer agency became popular. The following example illustrates a situation where the client chose to file against her agent for violation of Article 1, specifically Standard of Practice 1-4.

Article 1 Case Study
Representing the Client's Best Interests

Mary J. was preparing to purchase a home for the first time. She was very excited about the prospect of becoming a homeowner and wanted to be sure she did everything just right. After reading several articles about the importance of having an agent to represent your interests as a buyer, Mary began to scan the real estate ads each day to look for a property that might interest her and to locate someone to be her buyer agent. Jack M. had placed a fairly large ad that caught her eye with a lead line saying "Work with me as your buyer agent and save thousands of dollars!" Mary contacted Jack and quickly signed an exclusive-right-to-represent contract. Jack proceeded to research available properties that fell in Mary's price range and they started looking at houses.

The market in Mary and Jack's city had very suddenly turned into a seller's market (more buyers than listings available) and attractive, well-priced homes were only remaining on the market for a matter of hours. On the second day of looking, Mary found a place that she fell in love with. Jack advised her that it was entirely possible that there would be multiple contracts presented at the same time on this most desirable property and that if she were really serious about buying it, she should consider offering several thousand dollars over the list price. Fearful of losing her dream home, Mary took Jack's advice and made an offer $3,000 above list price. As it turned out, there were three offers presented at the same time on the property, all of them at list price or more, but Mary's was the best offer and the sellers signed a contract with her.

A few days after settlement, Mary filed a complaint against Jack with the local association of REALTORS® citing Article 1, Standards of Practice 1-4 which clearly states that a REALTOR® should not mislead buyers into thinking they will realize savings by working with that particular buyer agent. Mary argued that instead of saving thousands of dollars as promised in the ad, she had in fact spent an additional $3,000!

***

Article 2. The second most cited article is Article 2 which states that a REALTOR® must avoid exaggeration, misrepresentation or concealment of pertinent facts relating to the property or the transaction. It further states that the REALTOR® is not responsible for disclosure of latent defects, advising on matters outside the scope of the real estate license or disclosure of facts that are considered to be confidential under state law.

One of a real estate agent's worst nightmares is receiving a frantic call from the new owners of a property that settled ten days ago screaming that the basement has flooded and that it is all the agent's fault! Broken-down air conditioning systems when it is 100 degrees in the shade, overflowing dishwashers, stopped-up chimneys, the list goes on. In most states, license law requires disclosure of all **adverse material defects** in a property—things that affect the normal function and operation of residence, for example, a leaking roof or malfunctioning stove. In addition to license law, disclosure is also mandated in agency law, and in many states there is a required seller disclosure form. Plus, today's agents strongly recommend that the purchasers include a contingency clause in the contract allowing for a professional home inspection to be made immediately after a purchase contract is accepted. In spite of all this, occasionally things will go wrong after closing. The sellers swear it never happened when they lived there, the agent reminds the purchaser that they had a thorough home inspection, but the case may still end up in the hands of the Grievance Committee.

Nonmaterial defects. Some of the more interesting cases involving Article 2 are those where a complaint is filed for lack of disclosure of nonmaterial defects. A property in which a suicide, rape or murder has occurred or one that is said to be haunted by ghosts is often referred to as a **stigmatized property.** State laws vary as to the necessity to disclose such information. The Code clearly states that no disclosure is required, but agents may find themselves with their own ethical dilemma over how much information should be disclosed to the buyer.

Articles Most Often Found in Violation

Although Articles 1 and 2 are the ones most often cited in a complaint, Articles 9 and 12 are the ones where REALTORS® have most often been found to have been in violation.

Article 9. Article 9 very simply states that all agreements shall be in writing in clear and understandable language expressing the specific terms, conditions, obligations and commitments of the parties. Meeting this obligation should be easily achieved, especially with the convenience of fax machines, which may be found almost everywhere today.

Unfortunately, agents, buyers and sellers continue to make oral agreements that often lead to misunderstanding and problems later on. The problem is not usually with the initial offer to purchase or even with counteroffers made during the original negotiation for the property. The problems tend to arise over things like resolution of home inspection repair or replacement requests, misunderstanding about items to either convey or not convey with the property, or changes in the proposed settlement date that occur after the original contract has been agreed upon.

Article 12. Article 12 cautions REALTORS® to be careful to always present a true picture in their advertising. If an agent wishes to advertise a "free microwave to every buyer that works with me," the agent must make it very clear exactly what is required before that buyer will receive the promised microwave. Presumably the agent means the buyer will receive a microwave at the time of closing, but the ad could be construed to mean that someone just spending a day or two out looking at property with the agent could get in line for the free microwave!

At one time, the offering of premiums, prizes or discounts as an inducement to list or purchase with a particular agent was considered to be unethical behavior. In 1995 Standard of Practice 12-3 was amended to indicate that the such an offering is not in and of itself unethical as long as all the terms and conditions of the offer are clearly stated.

Fiduciary responsibility. Prior to the advent of buyer agency, all real estate agents owed the duties of care, obedience, accounting and loyalty, what is termed a **fiduciary responsibility**, to the seller; in fact the agents on *both* sides of the transaction worked on behalf of the seller. As a result, only the listing agent was allowed to advertise that he or she had "sold" the property. As buyer agency became popular in the mid-90s, Standard of Practice 12-7 was amended to allow both agents involved in the transaction to advertise they had sold the property.

Article 16. Article 16, only four lines long, states that a REALTOR® shall not engage in any practice that might interfere with the agency relationship of another REALTOR® with his or her client. Although this Article may be short it is apparently far from sweet. There are 20 Standards of Practice attached to this Article, almost all of them adopted or amended since 1993.

The Standards of Practice cover a wide range of subjects, including an interpretation of how telephone or mail solicitations may be made ethically, admonitions to never solicit a listing currently listed with another broker, and a prohibition against inducing clients a REALTOR® represents to leave the current broker and join the agent when they move to a different firm.

Article 16 Case Study
Interfering with Another Agent's Brokerage Relationship

When a local market suddenly turns into a "seller's market" where there are many buyers but few desirable listings a situation such as given in the following example could easily place a REALTOR® in a potentially unethical situation.

Helen R. just listed a house in almost perfect condition in a very popular part of town and is holding it open on Sunday afternoon. By four o'clock more than two dozen people have visited the property and many of them have expressed a definite interest. A little after four, Mark W. comes in. Helen asks Mark if he has a agent to represent him and he indicates that he does but that his buyer agent is out of town attending his daughter's wedding that afternoon and could not come with him. Mark has been looking at properties for about two weeks and immediately knows that this is the perfect house for him and his family.

Helen reminds Mark that she represents the seller but cautions him that this house will certainly not remain on the market very long. She tells him that several others that have come to the open house that afternoon have indicated that they intend to make an offer and that if he is definitely interested perhaps he should consider having her write up the offer right now. She explains that she can write the offer for Mark, treating him as a customer rather than as a client.

Concerned that he may not be able to contact his own agent until much later and anxious that he not miss out on the chance to purchase the property, Mark agrees to have Helen write the contract. Mark's offer is accepted and settlement is scheduled for 30 days from now. Did Helen interfere with the agency relationship Mark has with his own agent? Was Helen acting in the best interests of her client, the seller? or in Mark's? or in her own?

SUMMARY

From the early days of unscrupulous land agents selling desert land in the west to the characters portrayed in present day movies, those who participate in the buying and selling of real property have suffered from a poor public image. Gallup polls consistently show real estate agents ranked close to the bottom of the list of trusted professions and occupations. The National Association of REALTORS® is working to improve this image with a TV campaign endeavoring to increase public awareness of what value the REALTOR® brings to the transaction.

Every member of the National Association of REALTORS® is pledged to follow the REALTOR® Code of Ethics that was written in 1913 and is reviewed and updated every year. The 17 Articles of the Code plus accompanying Standards of Practice set a level of ethical behavior for all members of the association.

Members of the public and other REALTORS® may file a complaint citing violation of one or more of the Articles of the Code. REALTORS® found in violation of the code are subject to reprimand, fine, or expulsion. A formal set of procedures is mandated in all cases of either ethics or arbitration complaints to insure that all parties receive fair due process.

Article 1 (protecting the best interests of the client) and Article 2 (providing proper disclosures) are the articles most often cited in complaints. Article 9 (have all agreements in writing) and Article 12 (presenting a true picture in advertising) are the ones most often actually found to be in violation.

Chapter 2 / National Association of REALTORS® Code of Ethics

Quiz

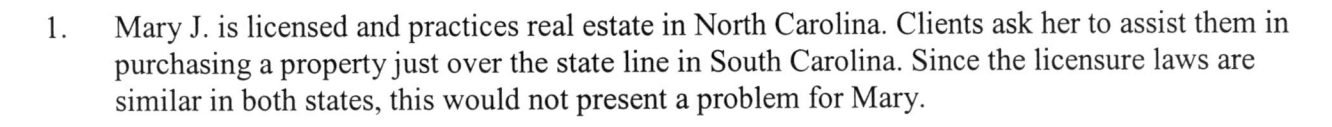

1. Mary J. is licensed and practices real estate in North Carolina. Clients ask her to assist them in purchasing a property just over the state line in South Carolina. Since the licensure laws are similar in both states, this would not present a problem for Mary.

    a. True
    b. False

2. The annual Gallup Poll has shown that real estate agents are steadily moving up in order of ranking into the most trusted professions.

    a. True
    b. False

3. The Eastern European Real Property Foundation was created to promote more foreign investment in the United States.

    a. True
    b. False

4. Any real estate licensee that has the designation of REALTOR® is a member of the National Association of REALTORS® and has pledged to follow the REALTOR® Code of Ethics.

    a. True
    b. False

5. Each Article of the Code of Ethics includes numerous Standards of Practice to provide further illustration of how the Article applies in business practice.

    a. True
    b. False

6. The role of the Grievance Committee is to

    a. decide which Article has been violated.
    b. set the sanction to be applied for the violation.
    c. determine whether the complaint should be referred to a Profession Standards hearing.
    d. represent the complainant at the hearing.

7. Article 1 is the article most often cited in ethics complaints. In Article 1 the REALTOR® pledges to

    a. have all aspects of the transaction in writing.
    b. present a true picture in advertising.
    c. make full disclosure of all adverse material facts.
    d. protect the best interests of the client.

8. Three months after moving in, the Jones family suffers damage from a severe leak in the roof. They plan to file a complaint against the listing agent based on

    a. Article 1.
    b. Article 2.
    c. Article 9.
    d. Article 12.

9. Article 9 would most likely be cited in which of the following situations?

    a. Buyers discover a cracked chimney after settlement.
    b. The selling agent advertises she has "sold" the property.
    c. The sellers orally agreed to leave the washer/dryer but removed them.
    d. The listing agent refused to present an offer to the sellers.

10. Based on Article 16, a REALTOR® should never interfere with the agency relationship of another REALTOR® with their client. Which of the following situations might lead to a complaint being filed?

    a. Mr. and Mrs. Baker have their house listed with Jack W. but they have called Sally M. to discuss re-listing the property with her.
    b. Sally knows that the Bakers' property is listed with Jack but calls them to discuss listing with her after Jack's listing has expired.
    c. Jack W. knows that the Bakers are not happy with him and suggests that they call his colleague Sally to discuss re-listing the property with her.
    d. Sally calls Jack and asks for permission to contact the Bakers.

A Blueprint for Decision Making

3

LEARNING OBJECTIVES
After completing this chapter, you will be able to:

✓ Recognize the difference between an actual and a potential conflict of interest.
✓ Explain the best way to organize for making ethical decisions.
✓ Describe the four dilemma paradigms of right vs. right.
✓ Layout an ethical dilemma according to the blueprint for making ethical decisions.
✓ List the guidelines used to support or reject possible solutions.

KEY TERMS

actual conflict of interest
blueprint
dilemma paradigms
ethics committee
Megan's Law
ombudsperson
potential conflict of interest
whistle-blower

DETERMINING A CONFLICT OF INTEREST

An **actual conflict of interest** occurs whenever someone is in a situation where he or she has a personal interest in the outcome of a decision. The concern is that the person making the decision might be influenced by the personal benefit to be gained as a result of the decision. Take the following example:

> The brokerage firm has asked the branch managers to vote on whether to increase the advertising budget for all offices or to raise the branch manager salaries by 10 percent. The managers are asked to vote for or against a raise in their own salaries.

A **potential conflict of interest** occurs whenever it is possible that there may be a perception that the decision maker is more influenced by his or her own personal interest than by the objective facts of the situation. For instance:

> The sales associates in each office may perceive that the managers in the above example are making a financial decision based on the benefit to themselves rather than a decision that would benefit the entire office. There may in fact be substantial evidence that an increase in manager salaries would provide more of a benefit to the sales associates than increased advertising; that is, it might

attract better managers or provide incentive to current managers to work harder or to spend more time in counseling and coaching the agents. But the perception is apt to be that the decision is being made for purely selfish reasons.

How to Handle a Conflict of Interest

Questions to ask yourself. Some questions to consider include the following:

- Are you confident you can make an independent, professional judgment as would be expected from someone in your position without being influenced in any way by any personal interest you might have in the outcome of the decision?

- Regardless of how sure you may be of your own ability to be objective, is there anything about the particular situation that would lead someone else to question your ability to make an independent decision?

- Would you hesitate to discuss your possible personal involvement in the situation with any of the parties affected by the outcome of the decision?

Easy steps to take to avoid a conflict of interest. Agents can avoid conflicts of interest by considering the following measures:

- Total disclosure of any actual or potential interest in the given situation.

- If it is not absolutely clear that there is no potential conflict, remove yourself from the decision-making process.

- Be willing to ask for advice from local, state or national association advisors or from a trusted colleague who may have experienced a similar situation.

What makes the decision difficult? First, it must be determined if there is actually an ethical decision to be made or is it merely a business decision? Take the following scenario:

A large brokerage firm has determined that there is too much "dead wood" in every branch office and each branch manager must reduce the agent roster immediately. Joan W. must now pick five agents to be let go. Does Joan have an ethical dilemma? Is there a potential conflict of interest?

If upper management has issued strict definite guidelines for which agents should be fired, Joan will merely be carrying out a business decision. If, however, the manager is given the discretion to decide which agents should be asked to leave, Joan may have a potential conflict of interest. Will she only keep the ones she likes to have around? Suppose one of the agents with minimum production is Joan's husband? What if one of the agents is the principal broker's son-in-law?

Prevailing moral reason to act. If ethics are more concerned with what is right and morals are more concerned with what is good, what happens in the case of a **whistle-blower**—a person who reports bad actions taken by a company? Normally, a sense of ethics would demand loyalty to a company, but what if there is something happening that seems to be more of a moral issue? What if the company is doing something basically wrong that is damaging other individuals?

Newspapers, magazines, novels and movies are full of real and imagined cases of one valiant worker standing up against the megacompany, often at great consequences to themselves. The company usually tries to pass off the whistle-blower as a disgruntled employee with a sense of vengeance but this is not always the case. Real estate brokerage firm cases may not be as dramatic as those seen in the movies or in best-seller novels, but there are examples of whistle-blowers. Consider the dilemma of Mark J., a real estate salesperson:

> Mark J. has been working with "Best for You" Property Management Company for three years. Unfortunately, "Best for You" has not been attracting new clients and has, in fact, lost several this past year. The majority of their clients are state department or military persons who have left the management of their property with "Best for You" while they are on overseas assignments and have little contact with the company during the time they are out of the country.
>
> In attempting to have a check approved for a forfeiture of deposit for one of his clients, Mark finds that the escrow account has been depleted due to the broker transferring funds into the business operating account.
>
> Mark has always highly respected his broker and has had no reason to question his business practices in the past, but he is sure that this represents unethical behavior. In fact, Mark believes that it is actually illegal in his state for a broker to withdraw funds from an escrow account to pay business expenses.
>
> On questioning the broker, Mark was told that it would not really matter because there would be adequate funds in the escrow account by the time any other client was entitled to a check. The broker planned to make a deposit to the escrow account today. The broker further explained that without the occasional use of the escrow account funds, the company might find it necessary to declare bankruptcy and close its doors. That would certainly not benefit anyone, including the clients. Surely Mark could see that it would be much worse for their clients, many of whom were out of the country, to suddenly find themselves without a management company.

What is the right decision for Mark to make? Should he report his broker to the state regulatory body or to the local REALTOR® association? Should he notify the clients? Should he leave the company? Should he do nothing?

SETTING THE ENVIRONMENT FOR MAKING ETHICAL DECISIONS

Upper Management

In any company, real estate or otherwise, regardless of size, it is imperative that the president, CEO, chairman and members of the board give full support to the goal of always adhering to high principles of ethical business practice. A formalized system for implementing ethical behavior of all those associated with the company will help a company reach this goal. It is often said the personality of a company filters down from the top. The value system and sense of moral responsibility of a company also starts at the top and affects the actions of every employee or associate.

Ethics Officer or Committee

Although some companies find having one delegated ethics officer is adequate, in most cases it is preferable to select three to five persons to serve on an **ethics committee** to determine whether a violation has occurred and to determine the appropriate ethical solution. Because ethical decisions are so subjective, it is extremely helpful and probably more fair to have input from several persons instead of only one when making a decision. It is also suggested that a committee, or hearing panel, always have an odd number of members. This will avoid any tied votes.

Ombudsperson

Having an **ombudsperson** is a relatively new concept in the human resources side of business practice. The ombudsperson is there to provide information on policies and procedures and to advise either of the parties involved in the process. An ombudsperson is not there to act as legal counsel or to make judgments on the merits of the case. Having the benefit of an ombudsperson's assistance might prevent someone from feeling he or she has been railroaded into a decision without being treated fairly. (The original term for a person designated to assist without actually representing was ombudsman; today's more politically correct version is ombudsperson.)

THE "RIGHT" VS. "RIGHT" DILEMMA

Whatever Happened to Black and White?

Few of us would have difficulty deciding between obvious right and wrong. The hard part about ethical dilemmas is that the choice is more often between "right" and "right"! And the decision becomes, who is more right, or what is the best right for the most people, or what is the greater right based on law or religious principles. Ethical decisions tend to come in many different shades of gray!

Dilemma Paradigms

Rushworth Kidder has a great book entitled *How Good People Make Tough Choices*, (New York: Simon and Schuster, 1996). In it he points out four basic dilemma paradigms where there is "right" on both sides of the problem, creating the need for an ethical decision.

The first of Kidder's paradigms is *"truth versus loyalty."* This paradigm is illustrated in the case of George, a real estate agent:

> George listed the Smith's very nice home on Maple Street for sale. The Smiths confided in George that they wish to move because the next-door neighbors have told them that their son is returning home to

live. Unfortunately, the son has just completed a 15-year sentence as a convicted sex offender. Since the Smiths have two young children they are no longer comfortable living next door.

This morning another agent presented an offer to purchase from a young couple with two children, aged two and five. The couple has asked if there is anything about the neighborhood that they should know. Although **Megan's Law** provides that all states must provide some means of disclosing the existence of released sex offenders into the community, there is no requirement for disclosure by the owners or listing agent. Is it more "right" for George to pursue completion of the sale in loyalty to his clients, or is it more "right" to tell the prospective buyers the truth?

The second paradigm is the *"individual versus the community."* The struggle to balance the needs of an individual with the needs of a community is explored in the case of Helen, a real estate agent who also serves as a representative in her city council:

All over the country the question is being raised and hotly discussed about whether a community needs more growth, slow growth, no growth or the newest phrase, "smart growth."

Helen J. lives in a rapidly growing section of the city and sits on the city council as representative of that area. As a real estate agent she is obviously interested in more development which gives her the ability to sell more houses. As a single parent of three children, she needs a decent income to provide for her family. As a member of a community that sees children attending classes in trailers, fire and police resources stretched thin, and transportation nightmares occurring almost daily she is concerned about doing the "right" thing as she is called on to vote on growth issues.

A proposal is coming before the council tonight that would allow the rezoning of Jack Miller's farm for a new townhouse project. The new project will sell out very quickly due to its prime location but could add as many as 300 families to an area already suffering from overcrowding. What's the "right" vote for Helen?

"Short term versus long term" is Kidder's third paradigm, explored in the case of John, an owner of a real estate brokerage:

Where is the "right" decision to be found when John is considering merging his small brokerage firm with a large independent? The stricter standards and requirements of the new megafirm will probably result in some of John's agents being let go; a short-term solution would be to retain the status quo to protect these agents. In the long term, however, the increased market share and public name recognition should produce much greater results for the remaining agents in the company. How can John make his decision?

Kidder's fourth paradigm is *"justice versus mercy."* Everyone would agree that laws and rules and regulations must be followed, but are there ever extenuating circumstances? Consider the case of Annie, a new real estate agent:

> Annie just received her real estate license and affiliated with a medium-sized brokerage firm in her town. The brokers in her area participate in a multiple listing service with lockbox access to all properties for sale or rent. The rules are very strict about never allowing anyone to use a lockbox key except the person to whom it is assigned. Annie, not realizing the importance of this restriction, asked Joe if she could borrow his key because she had potential buyers for one of his listings. Annie was having trouble coming up with the money for all the various fees involved in getting started in the business and had not yet been able to afford obtaining her own lockbox key. Joe, anxious to have his listing sold, and sympathetic to a new agent just struggling to get started, allowed her to use his key. The rules are clear that both Annie and Joe should be punished. Is there any room for mercy in this situation?

Using the Paradigms

Most dilemmas relating to ethics will fit into one of the four basic paradigms. The persons involved in resolving such a dilemma may find it helpful to determine which of the paradigms applies to a given case. Using the paradigms will often assist the decision makers to focus on the true issues of the dilemma before trying to proceed with finding a solution. Recognizing that most ethical dilemmas will never have clear black and white answers may also eliminate some of the frustration when both sides appear to be "right."

THE BLUEPRINT

Just as an architectural blueprint provides guidance for the builder, a **blueprint** for making an ethical decision could assist the decision maker. Using the example of Annie and Joe and the lockbox key, we can lay out the foundation for the dilemma facing Michael, their broker, who must make an ethical decision in this case.

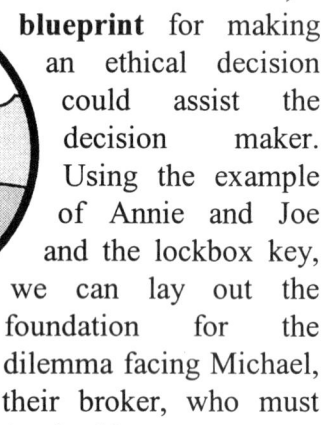

Laying It Out

The dimensions. Determine the exact nature of the problem. Is it truly a question or ethics, or merely a business decision? Is there more than one issue at stake? Who are the parties involved?

The problem is definitely an ethical question; a business decision could be to let all agents in an office use the same key, but this is against the local REALTOR® association rules and regulations.

The issues at stake are

- adhering to the rule against letting another use your key,
- protecting the best interest of the client,
- supporting the company policy and
- abiding by local association policy.

The parties involved are

- Annie, the new agent,
- Annie's buyer clients,
- Joe, agent loaning Annie his key,
- Joe's seller clients,
- Annie and Joe's broker and
- the local REALTOR® association.

Weed out nonpertinent facts in the case, disregard superfluous information that has no bearing on the problem and eliminate speculation or emotional responses.

Pertinent facts

- Joe has a property listed for sale.
- Annie wished to show Joe's listing to potential buyers.
- Annie did not have a lockbox key.
- Annie asked to use Joe's lockbox key.
- The local association prohibits loaning of key.
- Joe allowed Annie borrow the key.
- Annie showed the property to her clients.

Annie's financial problems and Joe's sympathy for the new agent are more connected with why it happened, and not what actually happened and could be considered non-pertinent. However, they may be factors that could justify mercy. The fact that Joe's sellers are desperate to sell is superfluous. The fact that Annie's buyers may wish to purchase the house makes no difference.

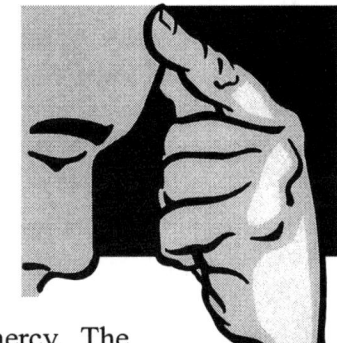

Decide whose problem it is—an individual's, the company's, the entire industry or even society itself?

- It is an individual problem for Annie and Joe.
- It is a company problem for their broker.
- It is not an industry problem. The fact that it is costly to become a real estate agent is immaterial.

The structure. Check what outside influences may affect the decision, or be affected by the decision—for example, state laws, the economy and cultural differences.

- The local association regulations prohibit the use of an agent's lockbox key by another person.
- Joe and Annie's company has a company policy that forbids loaning a lockbox key to anyone.

Specify who is involved—who stands to gain, who may be hurt. Is this a win/win or a win/lose situation?

- Annie may decide to quit real estate if punished.
- Joe may be angry with decision and leave the company.
- Joe's seller may be hurt if buyers walk away due to the conflict.
- Annie's buyers could lose a property they really want.
- The broker could lose one or both agents and two sets of clients; could be penalized by the local association; and could face resentment from other agents in the office.
- The local association could lose credibility by allowing a break of the rule.

There is potential for a lose/lose situation if the agents and broker are all punished and the house is not sold. There is potential for lose for the agents/win for the clients if the agents and broker are punished but the sale goes through.

Take into consideration what each party wishes to see as the outcome.

- Annie wants to sell the house and not be punished.
- Joe wants to sell his clients' house and not be punished.
- The broker wants to sell the company listing; wants to keep an experienced agent; wants to teach new agent a lesson; and wants to maintain respect from agents in his office.
- Annie's clients want to buy the house.
- Joe's clients want to sell the house.

Drafting Possible Solutions

Things to take into account. Which one or more of the four paradigms is apparent in this case?

1. Truth vs. loyalty
2. Individual vs. community
3. Short-term vs. long-term
4. Justice vs. mercy

Determine a best- and a worst-case scenario for each of the parties involved.

> A quick answer for a best-case scenario for both agents might appear to be no punishment and sale of the house. In the long term, however, could this actually turn out to be a worst-case scenario? Would Annie enter the business believing that rules do not really matter? Would Joe decide he always has the option of choosing when a rule must be followed and when it could be broken?

Would overlooking this violation of the rules diminish the respect other agents have for the broker? How would other agents in the association look at the actions of both agents and broker? What affect would this have on the overall morale of the office? Would the broker be looked at as a sympathetic good guy or a wimp?

Could this situation have an effect of the broker's membership in the local association?

Reviewing the best- and worst-case scenarios, consider who will gain and who will lose from the decision.

> In addition to potential gain or loss for the agents and the broker, if the conflict is disturbing enough to the potential buyers that they walk away from purchasing a house they really like, both the buying and the selling clients will lose.

Consideration must also be taken to determine if any personal, professional or religious values will be impacted by the decision.

> The personal and professional sense of ethics of both agents and broker will certainly be impacted, whatever the decision.

Investigate whether there are laws, or rules and regulations, that could later invalidate any decision made today.

> A decision that there has been no violation could be overthrown by the local association if the case is pursued further.

Guidelines to Help the Decision Maker in Supporting or Rejecting Possible Solutions

- Determine the consequences to the person charged, the complainant and those who may face similar situations in the future.
- Check on your own motivations: do you have any sense of loyalty to one party, or a sense of guilt for one side? Could you be getting even for an earlier action by one party? Or do you just want peace at all costs?
- How will this solution hold up over time? Will it serve as a good guideline for the future that will be considered fair?
- Are there similar cases that could be studied for possible guidance? A private conversation discussing alternatives with a person with experience on the same issue may be helpful. Your professional association may also have useful guidelines.
- Check on the legality of any decision including conformity with policy, rules and regulations and Code of Ethics.

The Final Drawing

The decision.

- Make the decision on how to resolve the dilemma.
- Put the decision in writing.
- Be prepared to defend the decision. (Be sure you are comfortable with it.)

Clean-up.

- Notify all parties in writing of the decision.
- Maintain a written record of the dilemma and the decision for possible guidance in the future.
- Accept responsibility for your decision. Even though someone else might have made a different "right" decision, you will know that you made your decision the right way and that it is therefore a good decision.

A Closing Thought

A quote from Dr. Michael McDonald, Director of the UBC Centre for Applied Ethics in Canada:

"After you make your decision, live with it, and learn from it."

SUMMARY

Whether the person responsible for making an ethical decision actually has a conflict of interest or is merely perceived to have such a conflict, there is doubt cast on that person" ability to make an unbiased, independent decision. If there is any possibility of such conflict of interest the best solution is to remove yourself from the decision-making process.

Setting the environment for ethical decision-making within a company starts from the attitude of the president or CEO. Decisions may be made through an ethics officer, or an ethics committee. An ombudsperson to assist the complainant may often by helpful.

The greatest problem in reaching a solution to an ethical dilemma is that there is usually some element of "right" behavior on both sides. Resolving the question of which is the greater right is always difficult. Rushworth Kidder suggests four basic paradigms that illustrate the problem of "right vs. right" that are helpful in laying out the problem

The blueprint for decision-making consists of defining the problem, determining the parties involved, establishing the pertinent facts, checking on external influences that may have an effect on the decision, and considering the potential outcome for all parties involved. Once a decision is reached it should be put in writing, distributed to all parties, and maintained on file for future reference.

Quiz

1. Broker Harold M. has been asked to serve on an ethics hearing panel. The complainant is charging one of Harold's agents. Harold finds himself in a position of a(n)

    a. actual conflict of interest.
    b. potential conflict of interest.
    c. no conflict of interest.
    d. codefendant.

2. Which of the following would NOT be a valid question to help determine a conflict of interest?

    a. Are you confident you can make an independent decision?
    b. Would anyone else question your ability to make an independent decision?
    c. Have you ever made a decision on a similar case before?
    d. Would you be reluctant to discuss any personal interest you may have?

3. If there is a possibility that you might be perceived as having a conflict of interest, all of the following would be recommended actions to take EXCEPT

    a. full disclosure of any actual or potential interest in the outcome.
    b. removing yourself from the decision making.
    c. asking for advice from a trusted colleague.
    d. proceeding with the case anyway.

4. A company will often try to pass off a whistle-blower as

    a. a disgruntled employee getting even with the boss.
    b. a union fight for higher wages.
    c. an employee acting from a sense of moral responsibility.
    d. an environmental impact on a factory.

5. An ethics committee may be preferable to an ethics officer because

    a. an ethics officer has too much power.
    b. input from several persons is important for more subjective decisions.
    c. more people in the company will be involved.
    d. it takes the pressure off the owner.

6. The role of the ombudsperson is to

   a. provide advice as to policies and procedures to be followed.
   b. act as semilegal counsel to one party.
   c. act as mediator between two parties.
   d. prepare the written report of the proceedings.

7. One of the problems in solving ethical dilemmas is that they tend to be

   a. black and white decisions.
   b. right and wrong decisions.
   c. right versus right decisions.
   d. no-fault decisions.

8. Which of the following is NOT one of Kidder's four paradigms of "right"?

   a. Truth versus loyalty
   b. Short term versus long term
   c. Faith versus reason
   d. Individual versus community

9. In developing multiple solutions to a problem, it is important to take into account all of the following EXCEPT

   a. best- and worst-case scenarios.
   b. personal opinion of the decision maker.
   c. who will gain and who will lose.
   d. any laws or regulations that may pertain.

10. After the decision has been made it is important to do all of the following EXCEPT

    a. put it in writing.
    b. notify all parties involved.
    c. accept responsibility for the decision.
    d. publish the results in a local newspaper.

Ethics and the Real Estate Business

4

LEARNING OBJECTIVES
After completing this chapter, you will be able to:

✓ Explain some of the societal changes that affect the real estate business today.

✓ Give examples of different styles of business ethics and how they may be illustrated in the real estate industry.

✓ Discuss the benefits of having a company code of ethics.

KEY TERMS

buyer's agent
Darwinian approach
glass ceiling

Internet
niche market
statutory duties

"young lions"

CHANGES IN SOCIETY AFFECTING BUSINESS

Changes Affecting Business in General

In the latter part of the 20th century, many changes occurred in the way Americans do business. Some of these changes have caused people to question old value systems or in some cases to reject them entirely. Constantly changing business ownership, diversity in the workplace and the age of the work are of particular significance.

Mergers, takeovers and buyouts. Every day we read in the newspaper about another business merger, takeover or buyout. Drugstores, banks, real estate firms, department stores and Internet providers are only some examples of companies that suddenly find themselves operating under a new name. Does bigger always mean better? Despite the inevitable spin about the benefits to be gained for everyone from the merger or buyout, many people remain skeptical. Customers are concerned that the new mega-entity will no longer provide them with individual service but will instead treat them as just another number. They question whether the same high ethical standards of practice that have long been recognized in the community will still be apparent in the new entity with headquarters in a distant city. They worry about what will happen to prices and service when there is no longer the need to maintain a competitive edge within the community.

35

There are many examples of the merger/buyout syndrome within the real estate business community. Especially in larger metropolitan areas, the midsize company seems to be disappearing from the block. As the costs of maintaining an office grow by leaps and bounds, the smaller companies find it more and more difficult to survive. There will probably always be a place for the small **niche-market** type of real estate firm that caters to a clientele speaking a specific language or belonging to one national origin. There will always be companies that concentrate on specialized aspects of the real estate market such as sales of hotels or shopping malls. Many commercial real estate companies tend to center their practice on their own local market. But the future prospects for the mid-size residential real estate firm are clearly diminishing.

Women in the workplace. World War II launched millions of women into the workforce that would never before have dreamed of jobs other than the accepted ones of teacher or nurse. Many of them were not content to return to the kitchen after the war, nor to encourage their daughters to resume the old accepted stereotypes. Women in the workplace have become an ever-increasing force to be dealt with. The last three decades have seen women become presidents, CEOs and chairpersons in companies all over the country. The proverbial **glass ceiling** (a term implying that a woman can never achieve a top-level position in a company) may not have been entirely broken, but it is certainly showing some significant cracks. The issue of sexual harassment has necessitated new policies and standards of behavior throughout the business world, including in the real estate industry. The important question is whether women bring a different outlook to the marketplace. Is there a higher level of ethical behavior? Is there more consideration for the individual? Will business be conducted in a kinder, more gentle way? Only time will tell.

Men predominated in the early days of the real estate industry, but it was soon found that women made very good real estate agents. Women were accustomed to taking care of others, to juggling multiple tasks every day and exercising patience. All of these are tremendous attributes for a real estate agent. Being a real estate agent offers a more flexible schedule than a nine-to-five job elsewhere. Women found this very appealing as it gave them the ability to earn a good income and also to be at home with the children when necessary. By the 1960s and 1970s the majority of agents or sales associates were women, although most of the managing brokers and broker/owners were men. The 1980s saw more women rising to the position of manager and today the numbers are about equal. Broker/owners, persons in high management positions within large companies and top elected representatives of professional associations are still predominantly male.

The age of the workforce. The management level of the workforce has become younger! They are not only younger, they have more education, and they demand higher pay. Thanks to the technology boom, young people still in their 20s have emerged as presidents and CEOs of companies. And they move around a lot! Gone are the days of looking forward to retirement with a gold watch after

30 years. One of the biggest problems for the emerging high-tech companies today is keeping their **"young lions"**—those college graduates with high technical knowledge, extreme drive and energy and a "take no prisoners" attitude—from quitting to take an offer for twice the pay from the company's chief competitor. What are the ethical situations that can arise from this dilemma? Where is the loyalty factor? Should employees feel a sense of responsibility to the company that brought them on board, trained them and gave them the opportunity to achieve a level that now makes them extremely attractive to the competition?

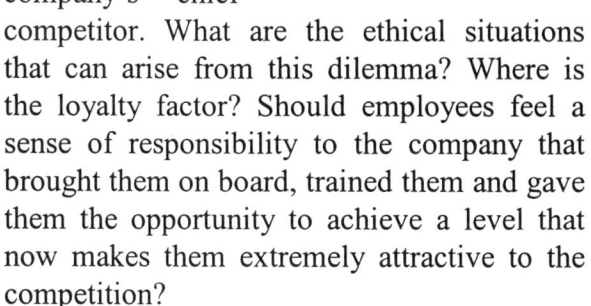

For many years, the average age of a real estate agent was in the late forties to late fifties. As we move further into the 21st century, this average age will probably drop. More young people today are entering the real estate business right out of college. In fact, several universities today offer a bachelor's, or even a master's, degree in real estate. One of the major problems for a young person who wishes to start a career in real estate is that real estate agents have traditionally been paid strictly on a commission basis. The lack of security in having no fixed income is prohibitive for many. Some companies today are addressing this issue by providing at least a minimum salary for new agents plus commissions based on production.

The emerging "young lion" effect is very evident in the real estate world in the operation of the multiple listing service (MLS). In many large metropolitan areas, numerous local associations now combine their efforts to form one large regional MLS.

The technology required to develop and maintain these systems becomes more and more complicated. Keeping the right people in these positions becomes more difficult every day as the techies are wooed away for higher salaries in other industries.

Specific Changes in the Real Estate Business

The Internet. "For more information, see our web site." How many times a day do we see this on TV, in magazine ads or in catalogs, hear it on the radio, or be told by a salesperson or other representative? You can plan your whole vacation on the **Internet**; plane tickets, hotel reservations, rental car, show tickets, city tours—you name it, all available at a click. Order the latest novel or hit CD, buy all the camping equipment for your next trip, research and select the best buy for a digital camera, camcorder, dishwasher, etc., etc., etc. Buy a car, buy stocks—all on the Internet. How does this new way of shopping impact the real estate industry?

For years real estate agents were in the business of providing information. Today that information can be found very easily on the Internet from many different web sites. The largest of these, www.realtor.com, can provide you information on over a million listings for sale all over the country. Every major franchise in the country has its own web site. Many individual agents have their own web site or web page. Today's real estate agent is selling service and expertise—not information. The consumer has plenty of other sources of information. The value of the real estate agent today is to assist a purchaser through the maze of forms, disclosures, contingencies, inspections and all the myriad details involved in purchasing a home.

Obtaining a mortgage loan. Most people need a mortgage loan in order to buy a house. Many lenders today have web sites with more information than most consumers could ever want or need about mortgage loans. A prospective buyer can even apply for and obtain approval of a loan through the Internet. There are many questions raised about whether the individual receives the same level of consideration and concern that may be provided by working with the lender on a one-to-one basis. Nevertheless, there are changes occurring in the ways many buyers secure the funds to buy a home.

A change in the way a buyer secures a mortgage loan makes a significant change in the way the real estate industry operates. Traditionally, a prospective buyer starts first with a real estate agent who will recommend several lenders that the agent feels will provide good service for the buyer. Will people now start with a lender first and have the lender refer clients back to a real estate agent? What is the ethical position here? Is it ethically appropriate for the lender who has now become the first point of contact to demand a referral fee from the agent? Another evolving trend is for the real estate agent to also be the loan originator for the same client. Could this possibly be a conflict of interest? There are no easy answers for these questions.

The global market. The use of the Internet and e-mail has had a tremendous impact on the move towards a more global real estate market. Business transactions can be conducted in seconds between offices located many thousands of miles apart. Real estate agents are signing up for courses in international real estate. Major U.S. franchises are opening offices all over the world. The collapse of the Soviet Union has opened the window for an emerging real estate industry in Eastern and Central Europe. The old adage about the three most important things in real estate are "location, location, location" has taken on a whole new meaning! The questions of what constitutes ethical standards of practice in a global market are just beginning. Accepting a standard of ethics that is concerned with what is "right" or "fair" does not necessarily mean the same thing in different cultures.

Buyer agency. Although there was always the opportunity to hire a real estate agent to represent you as a **buyer's agent** (that is, an agent who only represents the buyer in a real estate transaction), it was seldom done for two fairly significant reasons. First, if someone chose to hire an agent to represent them in the transaction as their buyer's agent, the buyer client would be expected to pay the agent's fee or commission. In most cases, the buyers needed their available funds for the purchase of the property and were not willing to pay the buyer agent. The second reason was that a buyer agent would not be able to show the buyer client any properties currently listed by his brokerage firm because all of the agents of that firm had a fiduciary duty of loyalty to the seller. If Mark J.'s company had the Smiths' property listed, Mark was responsible to the Smiths even though he was not necessarily their listing agent.

Early in the 1980s consumers and agents both became concerned about the liability involved when the agent was perceived to be working on behalf of the buyer while, in fact, the agent was responsible for protecting the best interests of the seller. This conflict in loyalties could lead to what is termed undisclosed dual agency, which is fraud. The potential ethical dilemmas are obvious, especially in the area of truth versus loyalty. During this time period, most states voted in legislation that required agency disclosure to all potential buyers. The disclosure forms stated clearly that the agent was working for the seller and required the buyer's signature attesting that the buyer understood that. If the buyer chose to hire the agent as a buyer's agent, the buyer would be expected to pay the brokerage fee. The ethical standards of loyalty and full disclosure to either a buyer- or seller-client were made clear.

In 1994 two significant changes occurred within the National Association of REALTORS® organization. Participation in a multiple listing service would no longer automatically mean that all agents should be working in the best interests of the seller. Previously, a listing broker would offer his listing through the MLS to other brokers in the area. The cooperating broker was considered to be a subagent of the listing broker and all agents involved in the transaction had a fiduciary duty to the seller. After 1994 a broker could offer cooperation for the sale of a property with compensation to either a subagent or someone acting as a buyer's agent. Since the listing broker offered compensation to the selling broker, the buyer would no longer be responsible for paying the buyer agent's fee. The buyer agent would be paid through the transaction itself. This made it possible for a buyer agent to have total loyalty to the buyer and participate in negotiating and promoting the best interests of the buyer client.

STYLES OF BUSINESS ETHICS IN REAL ESTATE

Just as a company tends to reflect the personality of the owner, it also reflects the business style of that owner which impacts the way ethical decisions are made and ethical dilemmas are solved. In a large real estate company these decisions may be made by a managing broker rather than the owner/broker. The managing broker's style may vary slightly from that of the owner or principal broker, but in most cases an owner will hire managers that complement his or her own philosophies.

There are various styles of business ethics to be seen in practice in real estate offices throughout the country. A discussion of some of them follows.

"By the Book"

This style of business ethics says everything must be done according the stated rules no matter what the circumstances. The "book" in the real estate business may come from several sources:

Legislation. Almost every state today has required agency disclosure laws that ensure that the public will know who the agent exactly represents. Many states have also passed legislation covering the law of agency as it relates to the conduct of real estate business. In many cases, the agency law prescribes **statutory duties** for agents—specific duties that agents must provide to their clients as stated in the statutes of the law—to follow in dealing with their clients, replacing the traditional fiduciary responsibility. Agency law may also include direction for duties to the party to the transaction that is not a client; strict guidelines to be followed regarding confidentiality; and specific reference to other legislation outside the law of agency that is mandated in a real estate transaction, such as fair housing laws, residential property disclosure laws and state regulatory agency rules and regulations.

Licensing authority rules and regulations. All states require licensing of real estate agents. The regulatory body also establishes rules and regulations that must be followed by all licensees within that state. License law extends into areas beyond the responsibility of an agent to clients or customers as stated in agency law. A section on standards of conduct (very similar to a code of ethics) is frequently included in the license law. License law also covers requirements for maintaining a license, punishments that may occur for breaking of any of the license laws, specifications for licensing schools and many other topics pertinent to the operation of the real estate profession within that state.

REALTOR® Code of Ethics. In a company where the principal broker is a REALTOR®, the sales associates are usually required to join the REALTOR® association. This means that the broker and all of the members of his or her office are pledged to adhere to the REALTOR® Code of Ethics. This becomes particularly significant when there is a dispute between two brokerage firms over which company is entitled to receive a commission for the sale of a property.

Article 17 of the REALTOR® Code of Ethics requires brokers to resolve an arbitration issue through an arbitration hearing panel provided by the local or state association. This is done in lieu of taking the case to court. It is a much less expensive way to resolve the matter and can be accomplished in a shorter period of time. In an arbitration hearing, the decision is made according the preponderance of the evidence as to which party is considered to be the procuring cause of the sale. An arbitration hearing is not usually scheduled until after settlement on the property. Every effort is made to maintain the clients' best interests and the brokers are careful to not disrupt the process that will lead to a successful closing.

"In the Long Run"

This style is mainly concerned with any long-term consequences for the company. The primary concern is for whatever provides the greatest benefit to the company as a whole rather than any one individual. Another aspect of this style is to take into consideration the effect today's decision may have on the company's overall image and reputation within the community.

"Walk a Mile in Another's Shoes"

This business ethics style is always more concerned with the individual. Consideration is given first to the effect on the person rather than the company. Extenuating circumstances will always be given great attention. The decision will be made much more by "gut" feeling than by strict adherence to any rules. The emotional response outweighs logic every time.

"My Way or the Highway"

This business ethics style is not unique, nor is it rare, but it is rarely ever successful, at least, not in the long run. This could almost be called a **Darwinian approach** to conducting business. Does Darwin's theory on the survival of the fittest really mean that he who survives must be right?

Case Study
Business Decision or Ethical Dilemma?

Top Hat Realty, a rapidly growing large firm in Big City, has recently purchased Tom Porter Real Estate, a small independent firm located in the southwest side of town. Tom P. has owned and managed his small five-agent office for almost 30 years and plans to stay on as manager of the new Top Hat branch. For years Tom has operated a very laid-back shop with outdated office equipment, no dress codes of any kind and no office hours in the evening or weekends. However, his little firm is well known in the community, Tom P. is beloved by three generations of clients, and the office is managing to stay at a break-even level (most months).

Tom's office does not at all fit the image of first-class, up-to-date professional service that Top Hat has worked hard to create within the city. Tom P. does not fit the prototype manager Top Hat likes to hire. Tom's agents do not look or work like the other agents in the Top Hat firm. However, Top Hat wants to create a presence in the southwest side and take advantage of the client base that Tom has built up over the years.

Depending on which business style the new owner prefers to use, the following would be points to consider in making a final decision:

"By the Book" Solution

If the "book" in this case is the annual profit and loss statement for Top Hat Realty, the solution may be to close down the office and expand the territory of another branch office nearby. Someone working by the book would say that this is a simple business decision.

"In the Long Run" Solution

Having an office operate under the Top Hat banner that is not up to their standards could be detrimental to Top Hat's image throughout the city, although closing down a small local office with an owner beloved by all could make Top Hat a villain in that community. Which is more important—the company's overall image or maintaining goodwill within the specific community? Is it ethically correct to always look to the long-range effect for a company's best interest?

"Walk a Mile in Another's Shoes" Solution

Tom P. has given his heart and soul to his business for 30 years. It would be devastating to him to be forced to leave. Besides, how much longer can he last? Is there a way to gracefully "retire" Tom? Would it be unethical to totally disregard the individual in this case?

"My Way or the Highway" Solution

Top Hat's CEO could issue an ultimatum to Tom to bring the office up-to-date technically, mandate professional dress attire for all agents and start holding the office open 9:00 A.M. to 9:00 P.M. weekly and 9:00 A.M. to 5:00 P.M. on Saturday. If Tom is not cooperative, he can be replaced. If Top Hat's CEO did not agree with the company policy in this situation, would he be faced with an ethical dilemma?

Benefits of a Code of Ethics to a Real Estate Company

Even an all-REALTOR® company may find it helpful to have their own company code of ethics. The REALTOR® Code of Ethics covers many different areas of ethical behavior towards clients and customers, the general public, and to fellow professionals. However, there are additional reasons for an individual company to develop its own code.

Sets a focus for the company mission statement. The very act of sitting down to formulate such a code is often the biggest benefit for the company. Being forced to take a serious look at the mission or purpose intended by the company is perhaps the greatest benefit in and of itself. Involving company associates in the process of developing a code of ethics and standards of ethical behavior gives a sense of focus for associates and management alike.

Helps in company decision making. Taking a lesson from the business world, look at the famous Tylenol story. Johnson and Johnson's decision to immediately pull millions of dollars worth of Tylenol off the shelves is often held up as a prime example of a company making the absolute "right" decision. In the short term, the decision may have been considered overkill. Tens of thousands of Tylenol pills, gels and capsules were destroyed unnecessarily. However, in the long run, Johnson and Johnson saved its reputation, and only two years after the 1982 crisis it was back on top for over-the-counter medication.

An important point to remember is that Chairman James Burke had earlier that year conducted a thorough review of the company's code of ethics. He has been quoted as saying that he feels this study is what helped his company develop the strategy to cope with the ethical situation presented to it and to make the right decision, regardless of cost.

Helps associates make decisions. Having a specific company policy or code may help give associates the backup they need to determine whether or not it is right for them to accept an expensive gift. The company policy or code may provide the associate with a gracious way to decline the fur coat or all-expense paid trip to Paris. "Thank you very much for the offer, but that would be against our company code" may be easier to say than "that would be against the law," or "that violates the REALTOR® Code of Ethics."

Establishes reasons to fire. A written code that all associates are required to pledge themselves to follow provides a basis that can be used as grounds for dismissal. In today's litigious world, brokers are often concerned about the possibility of being sued for telling an agent he or she will have to leave the company. If the agent has broken the state law or rules and regulations there should be no problem with immediate dismissal. The agent may, in fact, be subject to loss of license anyway. Very often, however, the violation is not that blatant. A violation of the company code could then be cited as grounds for punishment or even dismissal if necessary. As long as the requirements of the code are clearly stated, and there has been written acceptance of the pledge to abide by the code, the risk of litigation is lessened.

SUMMARY

There have been many changes in societal behavior in the last decades of the 20th century. Many of these changes are reflected in the real estate industry: mergers and buyouts, women in the workplace, the age of the work force, and use of the Internet. The advent of buyer agency in the 90s has changed many of the old precepts of real estate practice relating to multiple listing systems and responsibilities to clients and customers.

There are many different styles of business ethics practiced in individual business firms throughout the country. A few of the styles that are often seen in real estate companies are: 1) follow the rules, no matter what, 2) always consider what is best for the company, 3) show the most concern for the individual and 4) always do it the boss's way.

There are many benefits for an individual real estate company to have an established code of ethics. It will provide a focus for the company mission, will help in making ethical decisions, and will establish criteria for behavior.

Quiz

1. One concern about the growing trend to megasize real estate companies is that

    a. there will not be as much concern for the interests of the client.
    b. the cost of selling a home will rise.
    c. there will not enough agents to serve the public.
    d. many agents will become unemployed.

2. Some people feel that the advent of more women in management positions in the real estate business will lead to

    a. a lack of organization in offices.
    b. more discipline in the office.
    c. more consideration for the individual.
    d. shorter business hours.

3. Sally M. was hired right out of school by a midsize REALTOR® association to develop a computerized multiple listing service for them. After nine months the system was up and running to everyone's great satisfaction, but its success is still totally dependent on constant oversight by Sally. Sally enjoys her work and the association is very proud of her but is limited in the amount of compensation it can afford. Sally is being wooed by a competing MLS provider at twice the salary. Which of the following best describes the ethical dilemma facing Sally?

    a. Sally needs the extra money to pay off her student loans.
    b. Sally feels a sense of responsibility to those who were willing to give her the chance to succeed even though she had no experience.
    c. Sally is eager to accept new challenges in her field.
    d. Sally's newly developed system would give a real boost to the competition.

4. The value that a real estate agent brings to the client today is primarily

    a. providing information on properties available for sale.
    b. providing an analysis of recent sold properties.
    c. providing guidance and expertise in handling the transaction.
    d. providing referral to qualified lenders.

Chapter 4 / Ethics and the Real Estate Business

5. A real estate agent who also acts as the loan originator for a client may find himself or herself in a potential

   a. dual agency.
   b. conflict of interest.
   c. fraud.
   d. disclosed dual agency.

6. Performing to the highest ethical standards prior to the advent of buyer agency required absolute loyalty to the seller by the

   a. listing agent only.
   b. selling agent only.
   c. Both listing and selling agent
   d. Neither the listing nor the selling agent

7. George and Sally Smith purchased their first home in 1978. They loved their agent, Mary, and felt that she did a wonderful job of looking out for their best interests. In fact Mary was probably guilty of acting as a(n)

   a. buyer agent.
   b. dual agent.
   c. undisclosed dual agent.
   d. facilitator.

8. Broker Martin J. learned that his agent John T. has broken one of the rules and regulations of his state's license law. This was a fairly minor matter and did not involve any violation of the public trust. The state regulatory board has issued a reprimand and a $250 fine. Martin has told John today that he will have to leave the office. Martin is acting upon which of the following styles of business ethics?

   a. "By the book"
   b. "In the long run"
   c. "Walk a mile"
   d. "My way or the highway"

9. Susan T. is a new agent with John R's real estate firm. She was dismayed to learn that all new agents are required to take desk duty in the evenings between 6:00 and 9:00. The reason for this is that experienced agents tend to have appointments with clients during those hours and the new agents are more available. It is also an opportunity for the new agents to make contact with potential new business. Unfortunately, Susan is a single parent with two small children aged 3 and 5. She cannot afford a babysitter and has asked her broker to excuse her from this duty. When John agrees to waive this requirement for Susan he is acting from which style of business ethics?

    a. "By the book"
    b. "In the long run"
    c. "Walk a mile"
    d. "My way or the highway"

10. A real estate company's own code of ethics provide all of the following benefits EXCEPT

    a. a focus for the mission of the company.
    b. help in difficult decision making.
    c. criteria for dismissal if necessary.
    d. a plan for increased business.

Ethical Dilemmas in Real Estate

5

LEARNING OBJECTIVES
After completing this chapter, you will be able to:

✓ Describe cases involving ethical dilemmas that could occur in working with clients and customers and the questions that may arise.

✓ Describe cases involving ethical dilemmas that could occur with respect to the public and the rationale for solving them.

✓ Describe cases involving ethical dilemmas that could occur in dealing with fellow agents and the issues that are brought forth from the situations.

KEY TERMS

contingency	"fixer-upper"	ratification
counteroffer	FSBO (For Sale By Owner)	
disclosed dual agent	mother-in-law suite	

The case studies used in this chapter are hypothetical but are all based on real-life situations. After each case, there are several options listed as possible actions for the agent to take. The options are followed by questions to think about. Because ethical decisions are almost always many shades of gray, it is seldom possible to give black and white answers to the questions.

Use the four paradigms of "right" vs. "right" described in Chapter 3 to help define the problem. Review the styles of business ethics from Chapter 4 to clarify why certain actions might be taken. Put yourself in the place of the decision maker.

The quiz at the end of the chapter is based on the eight case studies.

Case Study #1
Is a Man as Good as His Word?

George M. was the listing agent for property owned by the Smiths. The Smiths' home was in very good condition and sold quickly. The Smiths then signed a buyer agency agreement with George and they began looking for a house that would meet their needs. George showed them a property he had listed that very day for $200,000. Since George already had a buyer agency agreement with the Smiths, he would be acting as a **disclosed dual agent** with responsibility to both the Smiths and the Jones, owners of the property that George had just listed.

The Smiths liked the Joneses' house and made an offer of $180,000 with two contingencies: 1) that a home inspection be conducted and 2) that the sellers would agree to repair the steps to the back deck. The Joneses agreed to the minor contingencies but made a **counteroffer** at $190,000 on the selling price. Because the sellers changed some of the terms of the original offer, they were now making a new offer (or counteroffer) to the buyers. The buyer's original offer is no longer valid.

The Smiths met with George on Friday evening to confirm the amount of money they would net from the sale of their own property. After reviewing the figures they agreed to accept the counteroffer at $190,000 but changed the settlement date to one week later. George called the Joneses to inform them the counteroffer had been accepted with one minor change in the settlement date. As it was now almost midnight, it was agreed that George would bring the signed counteroffer to the Joneses at 7:00 P.M. the following evening (Saturday). George could not meet with them earlier because he was to be an usher in his sister's wedding and would be leaving town early in the morning, returning in time to meet the Jones at 7:00.

At 9:30 on Saturday morning Mary B. brought her buyer-agent clients, the Browns, to see the Joneses' house. The Browns had lost out on two other houses they had liked by waiting too long to make a decision. They loved the Joneses' house and sat down with Mary at the kitchen table to write a cash offer of $200,000 with no contingencies. Mary called George on his cell phone as he was en route to the wedding to ask a few questions about the house. Since George would not be available to meet with the Joneses until later Saturday night, Mary asked if it would be all right for her to talk directly to the Joneses. The connection on the cell phone was not very clear but George said he guessed it would be all right. Mary met the Joneses immediately and presented them with the Browns' offer of $200,000 and no contingencies.

The Joneses were obviously pleased by the better offer but were concerned since they had agreed orally the previous evening to the Smiths' offer of $190,000. (Later they claimed they had assumed that the Browns' offer would be a back-up contract although that was never stated in writing.) They signed the contract and agreed to settle in two weeks. When George returned later that evening and was told that the Joneses had now signed a binding contract with the Browns, he confronted Mary and told her that the Joneses had already accepted a contract from the Smiths the night before. Mary reminded George that his contract had never been ratified and that hers was now the primary contract. (Final **ratification** is only when all parties have signed off on every aspect of the contract, including initialing any changes or corrections.)

Possible actions that George may take:

1. Remind the Joneses that a man is as good as his word and they had orally agreed to accepting the Smiths' offer the night before.

2. Agree that the Joneses had never signed off on the change to the counteroffer and were in the right to accept another offer, especially since it was a better one.

3. Plead with the Browns to look at the Smiths' position—thinking they had bought the house and then having it taken away—and ask them to withdraw.

4. Sympathize with the Smiths and ask them to look at the Browns' position—finally finding the right house after losing out on two others—and suggesting that George start looking for another property for them immediately.

5. File a Code violation against Mary for dealing directly with his clients, thereby interfering with his agency relationship.

Questions to Think About

1. What are the legal implications regarding delivery of a contract? When is a contract finally ratified?

2. Is there a question of agency liability in your state? What is George's main responsibility? Getting the best deal for his seller clients, the Joneses, or protecting the best interests of his buyer clients, the Smiths?

3. Should someone be bound by his word? Does "meeting of the minds" include oral agreements?

4. Who else was involved in the ethical dilemma? Mary? The Joneses? The Smiths? The Browns?

Case Study #2
Who Can Live in the Mother-In-Law Suite?

Bill C. has had a listing on Harvard Street for four months with little or no action. The house is in a very old section of town where many of the original houses have been converted into two- or even three-unit properties. The house he has listed is a single family, three-bedroom rambler on a fairly large lot. The detached garage at the rear of the property was converted ten years ago into a one-bedroom apartment accessible by walking past the house and into the rear yard. The present zoning will not allow this garage/apartment to be leased although it may be used as a **mother-in-law suite,** a separate dwelling place that is part of another property and can be used by a family member. Bill's seller clients are in their late 70s and very anxious to sell. They are both in need of assisted-care living and can move into a new county facility if they can sell and settle on their existing home within 30 days. If not, they will lose their priority and may not have another chance until next year.

Yesterday Bill received a call from Joe and Sue Green. They are very interested in the Harvard St. property. Bill showed them the house and arranged for them to meet with a loan officer right away. Joe and Sue really want to buy the house but they cannot quite qualify for the mortgage payments. Even if the sellers are willing to drop the price by $10,000, the Greens still need about $300.00 per month more in income in order to qualify.

This morning, Bill received a call from his friend Sally who works for a nonprofit affordable-housing group. Sally is desperate to find housing for Jim and Sue Miller. The Millers are in their 70s and have been displaced from the apartment they have lived in for 30 years due to renovation plans by the owner. Their combined social security payments would provide $400.00 per month for rent, but Sally cannot find anything for that price. She asks if Bill knows of any property for rent for around $400 per month.

Bill immediately thinks about the Harvard St. listing with the mother-in-law suite. The $400 rent would add $300 per month to the Greens' qualifying income. (The lender would probably count 75% of the rental income towards qualifying.)

Possible responses for Bill:

1. Do nothing since the Harvard street property cannot legally be rented.

2. Introduce the Millers to the Greens and suggest they work out a private arrangement for renting the garage/apartment.

3. Meet with zoning officials to apply for a one-time variance in the law.

4. Ask the Greens to find a family member that would be willing to act as the legal occupant of the garage/apartment but would in fact allow the Millers to live there, paying the $400 rent to the Greens.

Questions to Think About

1. Is solving a serious problem for two elderly couples more important than upholding zoning laws that are supposedly for the benefit of the entire community?

2. Would bending the truth in order to assist three separate families be justified?

3. Does the fact that the city never makes any inspection or other effort to check on the family relationship of persons living in separate units on existing property make a difference in the decision?

4. Does the fact that everybody does it (rents out parts of their home) in that neighborhood have any bearing on the outcome?

Case Study #3
When Are Three Clients Two Too Many?

Anne D. has a buyer agency agreement with Mark and Sally Jones. They are looking for a three-bedroom home located near public transportation into the city, a good elementary school and a detached garage where Mark can pursue his cabinet-making hobby. They need something in the $150,000 to $180,000 price range, but there has been very little on the market for them to look at in the past few weeks. Once or twice something has come up in the MLS, but they did not act quickly enough to make an offer.

Anne also has a buyer agency agreement with Helen and George Mills. The Mills originally wanted something with two or three acres of land but have now changed their minds. They have decided that something closer in with three bedrooms, a detached garage and accessibility to public transportation will be better. They cannot go over $180,000 in price and are anxious to move in before school starts.

This morning Anne received a call from Tom and Betty Green. They have just moved to Anne's city and have been referred to her by former clients of hers. They have been told that she is absolutely the best buyer agent in town. They would like to meet with her this afternoon to sign up with her as their exclusive buyer agent. And, by the way, they are looking for at least three bedrooms, good elementary and high schools and the ability for Tom to walk to the Metro station so that Betty will have use of their van during the day. They had hoped to stay around $150,000, but their friends have cautioned them that properties in Anne's city are more expensive and they may have to go higher. They are currently staying at the Holiday Inn and are anxious to find something very soon.

Sounds like a buyer agent's dream, doesn't it? Three motivated clients in a good price range—what more could Anne ask? In this case, Anne could ask for more available properties for sale. Her city has been experiencing a seller's market for the past few months where there are many more buyers than there are listings for sale, especially in the $150,000 to $180,000 price range.

Later in the day, Judy, one of Anne's fellow agents at Cooper Realty, tells her that she is going out to list a property that evening. It is a three-bedroom split-level with an attached garage located near the bus line that connects with the Metro. Many houses in that neighborhood have gone for closer to $200,000, but this house has been rented for the past five years and needs some cosmetic repairs like paint and new carpets. Basically it is sound, and Judy expects it will be listed at around $185,000.

Here are the options Anne is considering:

1. Ignore the new listing and hope it sells before it goes into MLS so she will not have to show it to any of her three clients.

2. Have all three clients come to the office and make a bid for the property.

3. Show the property in the order in which her buyer agent agreements were signed.

4. Call for "HELP" from her broker.

Questions to Think About

1. Anne is pledged to protect and promote the best interests of her client—but which one? All three are her clients. There is no law prohibiting an agent from working with more than one person interested in the same type of property.

2. Who should she show the house to first? The client she has been working with the longest? The client with the most sense of urgency? The client that is best qualified financially?

3. Should she tell the other buyer clients that she is working with three of them that might want to present offers on the same house? What should she do if all three want to make an offer?

4. One of the responsibilities of a buyer agent is to help the client strategize the negotiations for making an offer to purchase. How can Anne help any one of the clients strategize when she knows what the others are planning to offer?

Case Study #4
To FSBO or not to FSBO!

Bob M. has a buyer client that has spent several months looking for a **"fixer-upper"**—a property that is basically sound but that needs a great deal of repair work and updating. The client, Jack T., is a carpenter by trade and could do the necessary repairs but he works as a sub-contractor on an hourly basis so it has been very difficult to have him pre-approved for a mortgage loan. The one time it appeared that Bob had found a property that would suit Jack's needs, the sellers received a second offer with better qualified purchasers and Jack's offer was rejected.

On the way to the office this morning, Bob's usual route was backed up due to an accident, so he cut through a small side street. At the end of the street sat a small, rather dilapidated house with a For Sale sign in the yard. The sign was hand printed and obviously that of a **For Sale By Owner,** not a real estate company. Bob called the number on the sign from his car phone and asked if the owner would consider cooperating with a REALTOR®. The owner said sure until Bob explained that he would also ask for the owner to pay him a commission. The owner then explained that he already owes more on the house than he can possibly hope to gain from the sale, and that he is in fact on the verge of foreclosure if he is not able to sell the house before the end of the month.

Bob knows that there is no way that his client Jack can afford to pay his commission. Jack has been able to save just enough to provide a minimum down payment, and it has taken some very creative thinking on the part of the loan officer to find a loan product that Jack can qualify for.

Possible actions for Bob to take:

1. Forget about the FSBO and keep searching the MLS for something for Jack.

2. Tell Jack about the FSBO but do not show it to him unless Jack can come up with the commission.

3. Arrange for Jack to meet the FSBO and help them work out a contract.

4. Convince the FSBO to raise the price on the house enough to provide a commission for Bob.

5. Try to contact the lender on the FSBO property to offer to list the property after it goes to foreclosure, then sell it to Jack.

Questions to Think About

1. In the buyer agency agreement, Bob has contracted with Jack to help him locate a property suitable to his wants and needs. The contract further states that Jack agrees that Bob should be paid a certain amount for his services. Although the buyer agent is usually paid through the transaction, if there is no listing broker to provide payment to the selling broker, Jack would be responsible for the commission. But what if Jack cannot pay it?

2. Is Bob still obligated to show Jack the FSBO even though there is probably no chance that he will be paid? Is he failing to protect and promote the best interests of his client if he neglects to show the property?

3. What if raising the price to cover a commission means that the house appraises below the sales price and Jack is unable to obtain the loan? If this causes a delay in settlement, the house may go to foreclosure anyway.

4. Would contacting the FSBO's lender be unethical behavior?

Case Study #5
Is It Legal, Ethical and Moral?

John G. has had a long-term real estate business relationship with Mr. and Mrs. Martin. He has been the listing agent for them on numerous rental properties and, in fact, also sold them their present home. They have now listed a three-bedroom townhouse in an older section of the city with John. John has run several ads in the local newspaper, and the property has been shown once or twice by other agents.

Sarah D., another agent in John's company, shows the property on Wednesday morning and presents John with a filled-in application and security deposit check from Mark Brown and Susan Green. When John takes the application to the Martins to review, it is apparent that Mr. Brown and Ms. Green are extremely well qualified financially and have excellent previous rental references. It is also apparent, however, that they are not married although have been living together as a couple for five years. The Martins find this offensive and refuse to rent to them.

What ethical dilemma does this present for John? What action can he take?

1. Return the application to Brown and Green stamped "refused" with no explanation?

2. Agree with the Martins that they have the right to make this decision? After all, it is their property.

3. Try to convince the Martins that local fair housing laws prohibit this type of discrimination?

4. Return the application and suggest that Brown and Green file suit for discrimination?

Questions to Think About

1. What does your local or state fair housing law state regarding marital status?

2. Does a property owner have the right to make decisions based on their own personal beliefs?

3. What position should the broker take? Should the listing be dropped?

4. Should the Martins be reported to local fair housing authorities?

Case Study #6
The Web and I!

Sally B. has gotten very excited by all the great possibilities offered for advertising on the World Wide Web. She took a course in developing a personal web site at the local community college and spent several days experimenting with setting up her site.

Sally is a very active listing agent in the Brentwood Hills area and always has two or three listings in that neighborhood. She likes to feel that she is "the" agent for families in Brentwood Hills. As she was preparing her web site, she left space to advertise four listings from Brentwood Hills at any given time. Since she actually only has three of her own listings at the moment, she included one that Hal M. has listed in the same area. The page is entitled "Current Listings for Sale in Brentwood Hills" and shows a picture of the front of each house with several lines of information about the property.

The web site seems to be a great success. Sally has already received several very enthusiastic calls asking for more information about the houses shown. The next caller, Hal M., is somewhat less than enthusiastic. In fact, he is boiling mad! He stumbled across Sally's site when perusing web sites for houses for sale and recognized his own listing on her Brentwood Hills page.

Actions Sally could take:

1. Apologize profusely to Hal and remove his listing from her web site.

2. Hold her ground with Hal and point out that the ad only said these houses were for sale, not that she herself had listed them.

3. Call Hal's sellers and ask their permission to show their house on her site.

4. Call Hal's broker and ask if she minds if Sally runs the listing on her site.

Questions to Think About

1. If Sally is intentionally implying that all of the listings are hers, is she acting unethically?

2. Would there be no question of unethical behavior if she asked Hal's sellers for permission to run the ad? They might appreciate additional advertising.

3. Does the World Wide Web open everyone's information to everyone else without any need for permission? Hal's listing appears on his company's web site and on www.realtor.com.

4. Would Hal have good cause to file an ethics violation against Sally for interfering with his agency relationship with his sellers?

Case Study #7
Am I My Brother's Keeper?

Helen J., owner of J & J Realty, receives a call from Mr. and Mrs. Smith to come over to their house to discuss listing their home with her. They make an appointment for Thursday evening at 7:00 P.M. As Helen is preparing her background research for the property, she finds that the home is currently listed with Jack W., an agent with another company in town.

The Smiths' property is in a very good location but it appears to Helen to be about $15,000 overpriced. While meeting with the Smiths, Helen also notes that the living room and dining area are badly in need of new paint. If these two conditions could be corrected, it is a listing that Helen would very much like to have.

When Helen meets with the Smiths, she tells them that she had noticed that the property was currently listed with Jack W. although there was no sign in the yard. The Smiths tell her that they do not wish to continue their relationship with Jack W. and that they have removed the sign themselves. They do not feel that he has done a good job of marketing their property and even worse, they are very suspicious that he has stolen some prescription drugs from their medicine cabinet! They realize they have a signed listing with Jack that extends for another 30 days but they do not ever want him in their house again.

Although Helen does not know Jack personally, she recalls that another agent in her own company had worked with him a few months previously and had commented that Jack always acted like he was "high" on something. Helen's local REALTOR® association is very sensitive about drug issues today because several clients have complained that drugs have been taken from their homes either during open houses or property showings.

How can Helen respond to this ethical dilemma?

1. Sympathize with the Smiths, advise them on how to withdraw from the listing agreement with Jack, and relist the property?

2. Honor Jack's listing agreement with the Smiths and suggest they call her back when the listing term has expired?

3. Call Jack's broker and suggest he check into the situation?

4. Call her own broker and suggest he speak to Jack's broker?

5. Invite Jack for coffee and discuss the problem with him?

Questions to Think About

1. Where is the highest loyalty here? To the Smiths? To Jack? To the local association? To the general public?

2. Did Helen act ethically in meeting with the Smiths? Is it all right for her to discuss listing the property? Now, or only after the listing expires?

3. Are we responsible for the actions of fellow real estate agents?

4. Does the REALTOR® Code of Ethics address this issue?

Case Study #8
Can an Ad Go "Behind the Sign"?

Bill L. is one of the "young lions" that has recently entered the real estate industry. Bill graduated with honors in computer technology and communication and has returned to take over his father's brokerage firm, New City Realty. New City has actually been pretty much "old" city for many years, specializing in older properties located in the declining areas of the greater metropolitan area. Bill has come home fired up with energy and bright new ideas for marketing that he intends to use to really shake the foundations of this part of town.

One of his first steps was to have two large billboards placed on the two major streets leading into this section of the city with a larger-than-life-size picture of Bill with his hand pointing out and saying "I want YOU to work with me. I will SELL your home, not just LIST it!" He has also worked with a couple of music majors that he knows from school and they have come up with a catchy jingle for a 30-second radio ad that ends with "tired of having your home LISTED, work with me, I'll SELL it!" The ad runs on the early morning and evening news and weather reports. Bill's next move was to send out a two-sided brochure to the 5,000 houses in his target area. The brochure featured color photos of some of the nicer features of the area like the community park and the historic library building. Again, he stressed his theme of "Don't LIST it, SELL it!"

After about two weeks of this intense marketing campaign, the complaints start rolling in. Other agents who have houses listed in the New City area are protesting that his ads are a direct slur on them when he implies that they only list and do not sell. And his brochure has actually been sent right to the homes some of them have listed! The angry agents claim that Bill is "going behind the sign" and actively soliciting a listing that is already listed by another agent, which is blatantly unethical!

Possible actions Bill might take:

1. Apologize to the complaining agents, take down the billboards and discontinue the radio ads.

2. Tell the other agents to mind their own business and double his marketing effort.

3. Count the listings he has taken and the sales made and disregard the complaints.

4. Change the radio ad to attract buyers and send out a mailing to apartment houses.

Questions to Think About

1. Would the billboard and the radio jingle actually interfere with another agent's agency relationship with their client?

2. Is it unethical to send out a mass mailing even though it will inevitably go to some properties that are currently listed? (NAR Code of Ethics says no.)

3. Can advertising be aggressive and innovative without hurting someone else's feelings or sense of propriety?

4. Would it have been better for Bill to have taken a slower approach to his marketing efforts to avoid upsetting other agents in the neighborhood?

SUMMARY

The case studies presented in this chapter illustrate ethical dilemmas faced in a real estate agent's major areas of responsibility: one's responsibility to clients and customers, one's responsibility to the general public and one's responsibility to other agents.

Case Studies #1 and #2 represent dilemmas faced by a listing agent. Case Studies #3 and #4 concern the responsibilities of a buyer agent. Case Study #5 presents a fair housing dilemma and Case Study #6 involves the newest ethical dilemma of how to properly use the Internet in advertising.

Case Study #7 concerns one agent's responsibility with regard to another agent's actions while Case Study #8 describes a situation where one agent may be interfering with another agent's relationship with a client.

Each case study ends with questions to think about and discuss. Depending on different circumstances, the answers may vary greatly.

Quiz

1. If George in Case Study #1 (pages 47-49) is a stickler for going strictly by the letter of the law, his first action would probably be to

    a. try to convince the Joneses (sellers) that they should go with the Smiths' contract that they had accepted orally the night before.
    b. plead with the Browns to withdraw their offer .
    c. advise the Joneses that they have every legal right to accept the Browns' offer.
    d. recommend the Smiths start looking elsewhere.

2. If George's response is to try to convince everyone that the Smiths should be the ones to buy the house since they honestly believed it was final last night, he is acting from a style of business ethics that says you should always

    a. go strictly by the book.
    b. put yourself in the other person's place.
    c. consider the long-range effect on the company.
    d. push to survive at all costs.

3. If Bill in Case Study #2 (pages 49-50) tries to find some way to make it possible for the Millers to move into the garage apartment for $400 per month which would make it possible for the Greens to buy the property, Bill is most concerned with

    a. following the letter of the law.
    b. trying to provide a solution for several people's needs.
    c. getting zoning laws changed.
    d. obtaining more listings in the area.

4. In Case Study #3 (pages 50-51), which of the following actions would be best for Anne to take at this point?

    a. Show the property in the order she signed buyer agent agreements.
    b. Have all three clients come to the office and bid on the listing.
    c. Bring in her broker for assistance in the case.
    d. Not show the property to any of the three clients.

5. In regard to Case Study #4 (pages 52-53), the best attitude for an agent to take towards a FSBO listings is to

   a. never show the property to a buyer client.
   b. attempt to get them to list with you before showing the property.
   c. show the property and hope the FSBO will agree to pay a commission.
   d. resolve the issue of commission before showing the property.

6. What is the appropriate action for John to take in Case Study #5 on page 53?

   a. Return the Brown/Green application marked "refused" and hope no questions are asked.
   b. Refuse to work for the Martins in any capacity from now on.
   c. Report the Martins to the local fair housing office for discrimination.
   d. Inform his broker who will withdraw from the listing immediately.

7. In Case Study #6 (page 54), the only way Sally could ethically include Hal's listing on her web site would be to

   a. ask for Hal's permission.
   b. ask for Hal's broker's permission.
   c. ask for permission from Hal's broker and from the seller.
   d. ask for the seller's permission directly.

8. If Helen believes there may some truth to the accusation that Jack is taking drugs in Case Study #7 (pages 55-56), her best action would be to

   a. report him to the local association.
   b. report him to the police.
   c. contact his broker.
   d. discuss with her broker.

9. In Case Study #8 (pages 56-57), Bill seems to be approaching his marketing strategy with which of the following styles of business ethics?

   a. "By the book"
   b. "In the long run"
   c. "Walk a mile"
   d. "Survival of the fittest"

10. Which of the following resources would help agents and brokers understand the "right" vs. "right" conflict in an ethical dilemma?

    a. REALTOR® Code of Ethics
    b. Four paradigms
    c. Business styles of ethics
    d. Ten Commandments

Glossary

actual conflict of interest the person responsible for making an ethical decision is directly affected by the outcome of the decision

adverse material defects defects in a property that directly affect normal operation

arbitration settlement of dispute, generally financial, between parties

Arbitration Hearing Panel panel convened to determine procuring cause and resolution of dispute

blockbusting form of discrimination where a real estate agent attempts to induce a property owner to sell because members of a minority group are moving into the neighborhood

blueprint a graphic illustration of building plan

buyer agent the agent who represents the best interests of the buyer and who has a contractual relationship with him or her

buyout the process in which one company buys the assets (and sometimes the liabilities) of another company

buyer's market when there are more properties available for sale than there are buyers

client person with whom a real estate agent has a brokerage relationship

code of ethics a formalized set of principles of conduct for a specific individual or group

cold-calling session members of a real estate office meet to make calls seeking clients to either purchase or sell a home

contingency a set period of time in which some specified future event must occur (or not occur), or the contract may be voided

counteroffer a response from a seller that changes the terms of the original offer to purchase received from the purchaser

customer person involved in a real estate transaction that is not the client of the agent

Darwinian approach based on the "survival of the fittest" philosophy of Charles Darwin

dilemma paradigm an example of a conflict between two aspects of an ethical decision where there is "right" on both sides

disclosed dual agent   one agent acting on behalf of both buyer and seller with full disclosure and approval of both clients

dual agency   when both the seller and the purchaser are represented by the same broker

due process   following an established set of procedures to insure fair and reasonable treatment of all parties involved

Eastern European Real Property Foundation (EERPF)   an NAR organization working with USAID to promote development of a real estate industry in Eastern and Central Europe

ethics   discipline dealing with what is fair and right

ethics committee   a group of people responsible for determining whether there has been a violation of a code of ethics; an odd number of members on the committee is preferable

ethics officer   one individual responsible for determining whether there has been a violation of a code of ethics

Fair Housing Act   1968 legislation protecting public from discrimination in areas of race, color, religion and national origin; sex was added as a category in 1974; mental and/or physical handicap and familial status were added in 1988

familial status   a protected class under the Fair Housing Act to avoid discrimination against families with children

fiduciary responsibility   responsibility of an agent to provide care, obedience, accounting and loyalty to the client; replaced in many states today with statutory duties

fixer-upper   a property that needs a great deal of repair and renovation

FSBO   term used in real estate for properties sold by the owner with no agent

Gallup Poll   surveys taken on public opinion on various subjects by the Gallup Organization out of Princeton, NJ

glass ceiling   term used to indicate discrimination against women achieving high levels of responsibility in business

good-faith estimate   form required by RESPA to be given by the lender to purchasers that enumerates all costs involved in purchasing a home

Grievance Committee   acts similarly to a grand jury; determines whether if the facts as presented are true, there may be a violation of the code of ethics

home inspection   an inspection of all major components of a house to identify any potential problems; usually required and paid for by the prospective purchaser

Internet   a complex electronic structure of interconnected computers and computer networks (the generic term "Internet" refers to the network itself, the information available and the activities of the users who access the information using the networks; the World Wide Web is the system through which most users access the information stored on the Internet)

land agents   original name for persons selling real estate in 1800's

listing agent   the real estate licensee that has listed a property for sale

listing contest   a contest between members of a real estate office to see who can obtain the most listings in a given period of time

mediation   process where a professional mediator meets with the parties involved to assist them in arriving at a mutually acceptable solution to their problem

Megan's Law   refers to legislation passed in 1996 requiring all states to establish a system for notification to the public when a released sex-offender has moved into a community

mother-in-law suite   a separate living area as part of a property that may be used by a family member but cannot be legally rented

Multiple listing service (MLS)   an organized system where brokers in a given area make an offer of cooperation to other brokers to sell their listings

moral   relating to principles of right and wrong in behavior

National Association of REALTORS®   trade association for real estate licensees

niche market   a specialized focus on a particular national or ethnic group or type of property

non-material defects   defects that do not actually affect the condition of the house such as a murder or past suicide on the property

ombudsperson   one who acts in support of one party to a conflict, assisting them through the due process procedures

points   each point is one percentage point of the mortgage loan amount charged by lenders to increase their yield

potential conflict of interest   when someone perceives that the decision-maker may be influenced by their own personal gain or loss from the decision

Preamble   the introduction to the REALTOR® Code of Ethics

price-fixing   agreement between broker owners to set commission rates (violates Sherman Antitrust Act)

Professional Standards Hearing   panel convened to hear an alleged violation of the REALTOR® Code of Ethics

ratification   final signed acceptance of all aspects of a contract by all parties

real estate licensee   one who is licensed by the state to practice real estate

real estate professional   real estate licensee who may or may not be a member of the National Association of REALTORS®

Real Estate Settlement Procedures Act (RESPA)   legislation providing that the consumer must be made aware of all costs involved in obtaining a mortgage loan and closing on property by disclosure on the good-faith estimate form

REALTOR®   real estate licensee who is a member of National Association of REALTORS®

REALTOR® Code of Ethics   written in 1913 to promote high ethical standards of conduct for REALTORS® required for membership in the association

sanctions   actions taken against a REALTOR® for violation of Articles of Code of Ethics

seller's market   when there are more buyers than properties available for sale

selling agent   the real estate licensee representing the purchaser

settlement   the final closing of the loan and transfer of title to the property

Sherman Antitrust Act   Legislation prohibiting price-fixing and defined market share

Standards of Conduct   part of state regulatory rules and regulations for real estate licensees' behavior

Standards of Practice   further interpretation or amplification of individual Article of REALTOR® Code of Ethics

statutory duties   those duties and responsibilities specified in state agency law

stigmatized property   property where an event such as murder or suicide has taken place; also supposed presence of ghosts in the property

USAID   U.S. Aid to International Development; promotes economic development in countries throughout the world

undisclosed dual agency   when an agent has legal responsibility to one party to the transaction but is in fact, acting on behalf of the other party without disclosure

Glossary

whistle-blower someone from within a company who brings attention to irresponsible or unethical behavior on the part of the company

"young lion" term used to describe an eager, aggressive newcomer to the business world

Answer Key

Chapter 1 / An Introduction to Ethics

1. b. Ethical decisions are based on what is right and fair, not moral behavior.
2. c. Morals are the accepted codes and sanctions of a community; ethics deal more with what is right and fair.
3. d. Only disclosure of material facts about the property is required. The problem is with other issues that could affect the purchaser.
4. a. Agency law, regulatory rules and regulations and Code of Ethics all mandate that an agent protect and promote the best interests of the client.
5. a. Sharing is best learned in early childhood.
6. b. Many states will give extra time to students for whom English is a second language.
7. c. The Golden Rule teaches "do unto others as you would have them do unto you."
8. a. The Sherman Antitrust Act prohibits price-fixing and market distribution.
9. c. Case interpretations are published every year by NAR.
10. d. Office opinion will inevitably be split and biased.

Chapter 2 / National Association of REALTORS® Code of Ethics

1. b. Agents must be licensed in every state in which they practice real estate.
2. b. Unfortunately, real estate agents consistently rank very near the bottom.
3. b. The EERPF's mission is to assist countries in Eastern and Central Europe to develop their own real estate industry.
4. a. Compliance with the Code of Ethics has been mandatory for NAR membership since 1924.
5. b. Some Articles have never required further interpretation.
6. c. The Grievance Committee determines only "if the facts as presented are true, would there be a legitimate complaint."
7. d. In Article 1 a REALTOR® pledges to protect and promote the best interests of the client while remaining honest to all parties.
8. b. Article 2 provides for disclosure of all pertinent facts relating to the property.
9. c. Article 9 states that all agreements in a real estate transaction must be in writing.
10. b. A REALTOR® should never directly contact the client of another REALTOR®. If the client makes the initial contact, there is no violation.

Chapter 3 / A Blueprint for Decision Making

1. a. Clearly, an actual conflict of interest is involved since the complainant is Harold's agent.
2. c. This is not one of the questions to ask yourself; experience on similar cases would have no bearing on the present one.

Answer Key   67

3. d. A potential conflict of interest may be as damaging to the outcome as an actual one.
4. a. Sometimes it may be an employee acting from a sense of moral responsibility.
5. b. The decision reached is more likely to be considered fair and unbiased if a number of people is involved.
6. a. The role of the ombudsperson is to serve solely as an advisor on policies and procedures, not to act as legal counsel.
7. c. Most ethical decisions involve some right on both sides.
8. c. The fourth paradigm is justice vs. mercy.
9. b. Any personal opinion of the decision maker is irrelevant.
10. d. Decisions should be recorded within the company records and should not be made public.

Chapter 4 / Ethics and the Real Estate Business

1. a. Many people are concerned that the megacompany will treat clients as a number, not as an individual.
2. c. Women are sometimes considered to be more nurturing in nature.
3. b. The ethical dilemma is in how to handle the sense of responsibility. Answers a, c and d are merely facts that contribute to the decision.
4. c. Plenty of information is available on the Internet, but only a knowledgeable agent can guide a client through the entire transaction.
5. b. Some might question whether the agent was acting in the best interest of the client or for himself or herself in making the sale.
6. c. The selling agent acted as a subagent to the listing agent with full responsibility to the seller.
7. c. In 1978 Mary had a fiduciary responsibility to the seller exclusively but may have given the impression she was acting as a buyer's agent.
8. a. In Martin's opinion there is no room for extenuating circumstances, ignorance or error.
9. c. John is taking into consideration Susan's personal situation. Perhaps she can pick up other responsibilities during daytime hours to compensate.
10. d. Developing a company code of ethics is not a marketing plan.

Chapter 5 / Ethical Dilemmas in Real Estate

1. c. The law says no agreement is binding or enforceable unless it is in writing.
2. b. George's attempt will probably fail since Mary can either press for a "by the book" solution or use the "walk a mile" philosophy for the benefit of her clients who also wanted desperately to buy the house.
3. b. Bill's main concern is in helping three different families solve their problems regardless of outdated zoning laws.
4. c. Buyer agent clients are clients of the broker just as listings are the property of the broker. The broker is responsible for making sure that the interests of all three of these clients are served and will probably need to assign other agents to work with two of them.

5. d. If the FSBO refuses to pay a commission, there is still the ethical dilemma of the agent's responsibility to protect the best interest of the client.
6. d. The broker can no longer service that listing, but John does not have to sever his relationship with the Martins on other properties.
7. c. The listing is the property of Hal's broker who would have to clear it with the sellers before granting permission. Sally should never directly contact Hal's clients.
8. d. The best thing for Helen to do is talk to her own broker who may wish to contact Jack's broker.
9. d. Darwin's theory of survival of the fittest says he who survives must be right!
10. b. Being able to recognize typical styles of business ethics and study of cases from the REALTOR® Code of Ethics will help but the paradigms relate to the "right" vs. "right" issue.